The Scent of Empires

Chanel No. 5
and Red Moscow

Karl Schlögel

Translated by Jessica Spengler

polity

Originally published in German as *Der Duft der Imperien. "Chanel No 5" und "Rotes Moskau"* by Karl Schlögel © 2020 Carl Hanser Verlag GmbH & Co. KG, München

This English edition © 2022 by Polity Press

The translation of this work was supported by a grant from the Goethe-Institut.

Polity Press
65 Bridge Street
Cambridge CB2 1UR, UK

Polity Press
101 Station Landing
Suite 300
Medford, MA 02155, USA

ISBN-13: 978-1-5095-5492-8 (pb)

A catalogue record for this book is available from the British Library.

Library of Congress Cataloging-in-Publication Data

Names: Schlögel, Karl, author. | Spengler, Jessica, translator.
Title: The scent of empire : Chanel no. 5 and Red Moscow / Karl Schlögel ; translated by Jessica Spengler.
Other titles: Duft der Imperien. English
Description: Medford : Polity Press, 2021. | Includes bibliographical references and index. | Summary: "How the turbulent history of the 20th century can be read in a vial of perfume"-- Provided by publisher.
Identifiers: LCCN 2020051784 (print) | LCCN 2020051785 (ebook) | ISBN 9781509546596 (hardback) | ISBN 9781509546602 (epub)
Subjects: LCSH: Perfumes--Social aspects. | Perfumes--History--20th century. | Perfumes industry--History--20th century. | Manners and customs--History--20th century. | Civilization, Modern--20th century.
Classification: LCC GT2340 .S3713 2021 (print) | LCC GT2340 (ebook) | DDC 391.6/3--dc23
LC record available at https://lccn.loc.gov/2020051784
LC ebook record available at https://lccn.loc.gov/2020051785

Typeset in 11/13 Sabon by
Servis Filmsetting Ltd, Stockport, Cheshire
Printed and bound in Great Britain by TJ Books Ltd, Padstow, Cornwall

For further information on Polity, visit our website: politybooks.com

In memory of Karl Lagerfeld (1933–2019)

Contents

Illustrations

Extracurricular activity

It was never my plan to delve into the world of smells and scents, much less perfumes. Like anyone who crossed the border at Friedrichstrasse in Berlin before the Wall fell, I knew that the divided worlds of East and West were divided olfactory worlds as well. But other substances and subjects topped my academic agenda. I had no project in mind, no intention of trying to fill a research gap or produce evidence of a new 'turn' in cultural studies. My understanding of the world of fragrance was modest at best, probably in keeping with the average experience of a man who knows the bare minimum about soaps, deodorants, creams and colognes. My contact with this world was marginal and occasional, occurring only when I traversed the perfume section of a department store (usually on the ground floor and almost impossible to avoid) or passed the inevitable duty-free shops in the airport on the way to my gate. What captured my attention was not so much the scent, or the peculiar mélange of scents, but rather the light and sparkle of crystal, the rainbow of colours, mirrors and glass, and the perfect make-up of the women who were not staff or salespeople here but models, living embodiments of elegance. This glittering world with its endless gradations of colour and nuance always felt very alien to me.

1

And yet, I had a strong urge to overcome my scruples and venture into this special universe, even without prior knowledge of it. It is an act of self-empowerment, in a way, to take the liberty of writing on a topic you previously knew almost nothing about. Any concerns were overridden by an initial impulse that proved to be more than just a fleeting impression. This impulse was to follow a trail in the kind of pursuit that develops its own drive, its own pull, which is not exhausted and extinguished until the trail has been uncovered and the story has been told.*

In the beginning was a scent. It filled the air on every festive occasion in the Soviet Union – at the Moscow Conservatory, in the Bolshoi Theatre, at graduation ceremonies and weddings. The somewhat sweet, heavy aroma came to be associated in my mind with fairly staid crowds, polished parquet floors, luminous chandeliers, audience members circulating the theatre foyer during intermissions. I encountered this scent later on as well, in East Germany, usually at official receptions, in the context of German–Soviet meetings and at officers' clubs. My original thought was to track down the scent, maybe find out the brand name. Everything else just fell into place after that.

My initial research revealed that the scent was a perfume by the name of Red Moscow. We know the story of the wildly successful Chanel No. 5, but few know the history of the most popular Soviet perfume. As it turns out, both fragrances can be traced back to a common origin, a composition created by French perfumers in the Russian Empire, one of whom – Ernest Beaux – returned to France after the Russian Revolution and Civil War and met Coco Chanel, while the other – Auguste Michel – stayed in Russia, helped to establish the Soviet perfume industry and used a perfume known as Le Bouquet Favori de l'Impératrice as the basis for Red Moscow. Both perfumes represent the birth of new worlds of fragrance, radically different life stories, the cultural milieus of Paris and Moscow in the first half of the twentieth century, and the seductive scent of power that permeated two careers: that of Coco Chanel, who became involved with the Germans in occupied Paris, and that of the lesser-known Polina Zhemchuzhina, wife of Soviet Foreign Minister Vyacheslav Molotov and a people's commissar in her own right, who, for a time, was responsible for the entire Soviet cosmetics and perfume industry. Coco Chanel temporarily settled in Switzerland after the war, while Polina Zhemchuzhina-Molotova was caught up in the antisemitic campaigns of the late 1940s and spent five years in exile, where she experienced the 'smell of the camps'. Chanel achieved success in the Parisian fashion scene of the 1950s, while Zhemchuzhina lived in seclusion with her husband in Moscow and remained a fervent Stalinist until her death in 1970. And a side track in my research led to the 'grande dame of German film', Olga Chekhova, who was also a trained cosmetologist.

As popular as the perfume Red Moscow may have been, it had little way of countering the stagnation of the late Soviet Union and pressure of the global fragrance industry. But it returned to the market in post-Soviet Russia, and its very existence – much like the passion of those who collect perfume bottles – has become emblematic of a peculiar 'search for lost time'. Such a search is bound to turn up startling revelations, not least that the Russian avant-gardist Kazimir Malevich (anonymously) designed the bottle for the Soviet Union's best-selling eau de toilette before going on to paint Black Square, an iconic work of twentieth-century art.

There were long periods of research in which nothing much happened, but then another surprising discovery would propel things along again. When you rove the bazaars of Russian cities and start collecting bottles and pre-revolutionary advertising posters, you encounter amateurs everywhere who have turned themselves into experts. When you make a pilgrimage to the Place Vendôme and 31 rue Cambon to see the staircase where Coco Chanel presented her collections, you learn that the world of luxury is no less enlightening a subject of social analysis than historical studies of the everyday life of ordinary people. The boutiques and perfumeries on rue Saint-Honoré offer a glimpse of the grandeur of craftsmanship and boundless imagination of artists and designers. This book might never have been written without the inspiration of the great Karl Lagerfeld. When you visit museums and archives that you never would have strayed into otherwise, you uncover networks and personal relationships that only become visible in the light of a specific constellation – Diaghilev as a contemporary of Coco Chanel; Malevich as a contemporary of Tiffany, Gallé and Lalique. And when you poke around on the internet, you find that Red Moscow is not just a nostalgic collector's item. You can order it online whenever you like.

Every age has its own aroma, its scent, its smell. The 'Age of Extremes' brought forth its own scentscapes. Revolutions, wars and civil wars are olfactory events as well. The divided world of the last century can now be united and explored as a whole, *post festum* – by following our nose, as it were.

Berlin / Los Angeles, spring 2019
Karl Schlögel

The scent of the empire, or how Le Bouquet de Catherine from 1913 led to Chanel No. 5 and the Soviet perfume Red Moscow after the Russian Revolution

It all looks like a coincidence. Late in the summer of 1920, Coco Chanel met the perfumer Ernest Beaux in his laboratory in Cannes. The encounter had probably been arranged by Dmitri Pavlovich Romanov, a grand duke by virtue of his affiliation with the Russian imperial family, cousin to the last tsar, and Chanel's lover at the time. Exiled from Russia, he was now living in France.[1] Like the grand duke – who was a close friend of Prince Felix Yusupov, the man who had orchestrated the murder of Rasputin in the winter of 1916 – Ernest Beaux belonged to the world of luxury and the fashions of the Russian aristocracy. Previously the senior perfumer at A. Rallet & Co., purveyor to the imperial court in Moscow, Beaux had returned to France after the Russian Revolution and Civil War and joined the French perfume house Chiris in Grasse, which had purchased Rallet. In 1913, he had developed Le Bouquet de Catherine for the 300th

1 Le Bouquet Favori de l'Impératrice (1913)

anniversary of the Romanov dynasty, but the fragrance was renamed Rallet No. 1 in 1914, since an homage to a tsarina from Anhalt-Zerbst was not expected to go down well with Russian customers while Russia was at war with Germany. Beaux had taken the formula for this perfume with him to France, where he sought to adapt it to his new French circumstances. Presented with a series of ten fragrance samples in his laboratory, Coco Chanel chose number five, the scent that would later go by the brand name Chanel No. 5.

Tilar J. Mazzeo, author of an *Intimate History of the World's Most Famous Perfume*, describes the scene as follows:

There in front of them were ten small glass vials, labeled from one to five and twenty to twenty-four. The gap in the numbers reflected the fact that these were scents in two different – but complementary – series, different 'takes' on a new fragrance. Each of these small glass vials contained a new fragrance innovation, based on the core scents of May rose, jasmine, and those daring new fragrance molecules known as aldehydes. According to the legend, in one of the vials a careless laboratory assistant had accidentally added a massive overdose of this last and still largely undiscovered ingredient, confusing a 10 percent dilution for the pure, full-strength material.

In the room that day, surrounded by rows of perfumer's scales, beakers, and pharmaceutical bottles, Coco Chanel sniffed and considered. She slowly drew each sample beneath her nose, and in the room there was the quiet sound of her slow inhalation and exhalation. Her face revealed nothing. It was something everyone who knew her always remembered, how impassive she could seem. In one of those perfumes, something in the catalog of her senses resonated, because she smiled and said, at last, with no indecision: 'number five.' 'Yes,' she said later, 'that was what I was waiting for. A perfume like nothing else. A woman's perfume, with the scent of a woman.'[2]

When it came to the name, too – No. 5 – she seemed self-assured and free of doubt. '"I present my dress collections on the fifth of May, the fifth month of the year", she told him, "and so we will let this sample number five keep the name it has already, it will bring good luck".'[3]

Many years later, in a speech given on 27 February 1946, Ernest Beaux recounted his own experience of the moment in which the legendary perfume was born:

> People ask me how I managed to create Chanel No. 5. Firstly, I created this perfume in 1920, when I returned from the war. I spent part of my military deployment in the northern countries of Europe, beyond the Arctic Circle, under the midnight sun, when the lakes and rivers

exude a particular freshness. I always remembered this characteristic smell, and after great struggle and effort, I managed to recreate it, although the first aldehydes were unstable. Secondly, why this name? Mademoiselle Chanel, who had a very successful fashion house, asked me to create a perfume for her. I showed her a series with the numbers 1 to 5 and 20 to 24. She chose a few, including number 5. 'What should this perfume be called?' I asked her. Mademoiselle Chanel replied: 'I present the dress collection on the fifth day of the fifth month, meaning in May. So leave the perfume with the number it already has. This number 5 will bring it success.' I must admit, she was not wrong. This new fragrance has been hugely successful; few perfumes have had so many imitators, few perfumes have been copied as persistently as Chanel No. 5.[4]

2 Chanel No. 5 by Ernest Beaux, 1926

No. 5 was abstract. It no longer had any association with the traditional luxurious aromas of rose, jasmine, ylang-ylang or sandalwood, but instead pointed to something new: the chemical production of fragrance and the work with aldehydes, ingredients that would 'change the smells of an entire century' and 'make Chanel No. 5 perhaps the greatest perfume of the golden era'. This was not the first time aldehydes had been used, but it was the first time they had appeared in a prominent perfume and in such great quantities, creating 'an entirely new fragrance family: the family known as the floral-aldehydic, the term for a perfume in which the scent of the aldehydes is just as important as the scent of the flowers'.[5]

The venerable art of perfumery, which had not yet entirely dissociated itself from its origins in alchemy and soap-making, thus collided with the chemistry of the industrial age. Aldehydes are molecules whose atoms of oxygen, hydrogen and carbon are arranged in a very particular way. They are a phase in the organic reaction known as oxidation, when alcohol is transformed into acid in the presence of oxygen. Aldehydes are said to be synthetic molecules because chemists can create them in a laboratory by isolating and stabilizing them during the oxidation process. These molecules can create a variety of smells: cinnamon, the citrus tang of orange peel, lemongrass. However, aldehydes are fleeting substances that dissipate quickly before vanishing altogether. They intensify the aromas of a perfume and trigger reactions in the nervous system, inducing a 'tingling freshness, a little frisson of an electric sparkle. They make Chanel No. 5 feel like cool champagne bubbles bursting in the senses.'[6]

This is the effect Ernest Beaux had in mind when he sought to recreate the aromas he had experienced as he fled from the Russian Civil War, crossing the snowy tundra of the Kola Peninsula inside the Arctic Circle.

'In the snows of the high alpine steppes and the blasted polar tundra, aldehydes appear today in concentrations sometimes ten times higher than in the snows of other places. The air and ice in the frozen hinterland is sharper and more fragrant than in other parts of the world.' The stark aroma of snow and meltwater in Chanel No. 5 was balanced by an abundance of jasmine from the flower and perfume capital of Grasse, producing a sweet and exquisite fragrance with an equally exquisite price. 'This essential contrast – between the luscious florals and the asceticism of the aldehydes – is part of the secret of Chanel No. 5 and its most famous achievement.'[7]

There are a number of hypotheses surrounding the creation of Chanel No. 5. The theory that it was a mixing error on the part of an assistant is countered by the fact that the chord of rose and jasmine is perfectly balanced against the aldehyde complex, meaning it was the result of systematic studies. And the theory that it was inspired by the bracing arctic air is countered by the fact that Beaux had already used aldehydes in his Bouquet de Catherine in 1913, which was influenced by the popular Quelques Fleurs fragrance from the French perfumer Robert Bienaimé (1876–1960). The most likely scenario, therefore, is that Chanel No. 5 was a (modified) remake of Le Bouquet de Catherine from 1913, which Beaux had renamed and presented as Rallet No. 1 one year later.[8]

Chanel No. 5 is said to be composed of thirty-one raw materials. In the elaborate language of perfume experts who want to speak in a manner befitting their subject, the list of aromas might be described (or camouflaged) as follows:

The top note is dominated by the vividly fresh, lightly metallic-waxy-smoky aldehyde complex C-10/C-11/C-12 (1:1:1.06 %), with its typical echoes of waxy rose petals and orange peel. The hesperidic-citric facets are picked up and emphasised by bergamot oil, linalool and petit-grain oil. The heart note is spanned by an aromatic core of jasmine, rose, lily-of-the-valley (hydroxycitronellal), iris butter and ylang-ylang oil.[9]

Molecular analysis has 'unequivocally' proven the lineage of Chanel No. 5, but at the same time, the formula is said to have remained a secret to this day.[10]

Much about the perfume is shrouded in uncertainty, including how Chanel No. 5 developed from this point onwards. This has to do with the nature of an industry that relies on secrecy, as demonstrated not least by Patrick Süskind's novel *Perfume*. But its composition alone does not explain the stupendous success of Chanel No. 5. Many other things had to happen for this to be possible, as we will see. Chanel No. 5 is the product of what Karl Lagerfeld refers to as the 'Russian connection' in his homage to Coco Chanel, meaning it is more than just the sum of Chanel, Beaux and Grand Duke Dmitri Pavlovich.[11] Ernest Beaux used his original Russian creation as a starting point, but he went on to develop a clearer, bolder fragrance.

> It captured the scents of Moscow and Saint Petersburg and Dmitri's gilded childhood. It was the exquisite freshness of the Arctic remembered during the last days of a fading empire. Above all, for Coco Chanel, here was an entire catalogue of the senses – the scents of crisp linen and warm skin, the odors of Aubazine and Royallieu, and all those memories of Boy and Émilienne. It was truly her signature perfume. Like her, it even had a past that was obscure and complicated.[12]

The perfume 'captured precisely the spirit of the Roaring Twenties' and ultimately 'shifted the paradigm' of the world of fragrance.[13] There is no better expression of this paradigm shift than the design of the Chanel No. 5 bottle. The message it sends is that the era of flowers and floridity, ornaments and embellishments, is over and a new age has begun. Jean-Louis Froment, who staged a major Chanel No. 5 exhibition at the Palais de Tokyo in Paris in 2012, says this perfume is the embodiment of the 'quintessence of its time'.[14]

A 'paradigm shift' of unequalled brutality had taken place in Russia in yet another 'time of troubles' – a decade of war, revolution and civil war. In the midst of this chaos, factories were shut down and expropriated, their staff expelled and murdered, and changes in ownership led to archives being destroyed or scattered across the globe. Plants closed when their workers left for the countryside to find food, the supply of raw materials was interrupted in the turmoil of the Civil War and blockade, and the authorities considered discontinuing the perfume industry as a luxury sector altogether. Foreign experts had disappeared (Germans were considered 'enemy aliens' and fled as soon as the war broke out in 1914), and work discipline had collapsed, as had production. Large cosmetic and perfume companies, such as Brocard & Co. in Moscow, lost personnel; Brocard had employed 1,000 people before the revolution but only had 200 afterwards. Master perfumers and technicians fled, and factory buildings were repurposed. The former Brocard building was temporarily used to print *Gosznaki*, or Soviet paper money, while the successor to Brocard had to move into a former wallpaper factory. An opulent publication commemorating Brocard's fiftieth anniversary in 1914 shows that, at the time, the company had one of Moscow's most advanced factories and one of the largest perfume plants in the world.[15] It is no surprise that, in the general deprivation of the Civil War period – with paper in short supply and entire libraries winding up in the stoves known as *burzhuiki* – it was unthinkable that the impressive advertising posters that had made the company famous throughout the empire would continue to be used.

Private enterprises were nationalized and given new names. Brocard first became State Soap Factory No. 5 and was later renamed Novaya Zarya (New Dawn). Rallet & Co. became Soap Factory No. 4 and then Svoboda (Freedom) after 1924. The S. I. Chepelevetsky and Sons perfume factory was turned into the Profrabotnik (Trade Unionist) plant, while Köhler became Farmzavod (Pharmaceutical Plant) No. 12.[16] If and when production resumed, it was to focus entirely on the toiletries urgently needed by the population. The perfume industry thus returned to its origins in soap-making – at least for a brief time. Priority was placed on the needs of Red Army soldiers who required basic toiletries to exchange for bread during their food procurement campaigns in the countryside. Soap and perfume became precious commodities in the barter economy, in which a single piece of soap could be equivalent to a life-saving loaf of bread.[17]

According to Russian researchers, it was primarily the workers and employees themselves who were responsible for ensuring that factories threatened with closure were able to resume operations. A worker and member of the Bolshevik Party named Yevdokiya Ivanovna Uvarova was appointed director of Soap Factory No. 5 (formerly Brocard) and made a personal appeal to Lenin himself on behalf of her factory.[18] As a result, some of the valuable essences used by Brocard and other companies could be recovered and used to restart operations on a much reduced scale.

The materials left behind by Brocard and Rallet after the revolution and nationalization – the tools, machines and ingredients – were not the most important legacy of these companies. Their real heritage was their ongoing work and the knowledge and expertise of their specialists and managers. At Brocard (or Novaya Zarya), the head perfumer was Auguste Ippolitovich Michel, who possessed the formulas for Brocard's perfumes and knew how they were produced. Essential oils began to be imported again in 1924, and Auguste Michel set about composing fragrances. His first new creation was Manon in 1925. Krasnaya Moskva (Red Moscow) was developed in the same year. As described by the perfumer S. A. Voitkevich, it was composed of essential oils of orange blossom, lemon, bergamot and musk. The base note was alpha isomethyl ionone, which made up 35 per cent of the fragrance; another account claims that the perfume had sixty components, including iris, violet, clove, ylang-ylang, rose and ambergris.[19] Though the scent was created in 1925, it was not launched on the market until 1927, for the tenth anniversary of the October Revolution.[20]

For a long time, no one talked about Auguste Ippolitovich Michel in the Soviet Union, and his authorship of the fragrance was repeatedly called into doubt. Apparently even pioneers of the Soviet perfume industry who had been trained by him, such as Alexei Pogudkin and Pavel Ivanov, spoke poorly of the foreign perfumer. But in 2011, Antonina Vitkovskaya, director general of Novaya Zarya, declared once and for all that it was Auguste Michel who had 'created the famous Krasnaya Moskva'. She presented a bottle of it as a gift to Dmitry Medvedev, president of Russia at the time, saying: 'Krasnaya Moskva is a legend of Russian perfumery. A sample from 1913 was preserved in our factory . . . We give it to you so you can hold a piece of the history of Russian perfumery in your hands.' It was a vintage flacon of the original perfume that had been renamed Krasnaya Moskva after the revolution. In the Moscow Museum for the Art of Perfumery at the Novaya Zarya plant, bottles of Bouquet de Catherine and Krasnaya Moskva were exhibited in cases next to each other.[21]

In truth, the story is not so clear. While we know the details and trajectory of Ernest Beaux's life, Auguste Michel's biography is largely a mystery. Ernest Beaux, son of the head perfumer for A. Rallet & Co., purveyor to the tsar, was born in 1881 in Moscow. After studying and completing his military service in France, he returned to Russia in 1902 and became the chief perfumer at Rallet, where he achieved great success with his Bouquet de Napoleon in 1912, released to mark the 100th anniversary of the Battle of Borodino. This success was repeated in 1913 when he developed Bouquet de Catherine for the 300th anniversary of the Romanov dynasty. In 1914, the perfume commemorating Catherine the Great was renamed Rallet No. 1 for the sake of Russia's French allies in World War I. It was a modified version of this perfume that Beaux would present to Coco Chanel in 1920 after the end of the Russian Civil War. The information we have about Auguste Michel's life, by contrast, is scant and contradictory. Some say he was the son of a French perfume manufacturer who had migrated to Russia in the nineteenth century, but he himself claimed in an interview in 1936 that he had been born and raised in Grasse on the French Riviera. He said he had trained as a perfumer there and then joined Rallet in Moscow in 1908, where he was apparently poached by Brocard.[22]

It is very likely that Ernest Beaux and Auguste Michel knew each other, and that Michel was aware of the fragrances being composed by Beaux. We know for certain that both men were students of Alexandre Lemercier, the master perfumer at Rallet, and that both benefitted from the innovative work of the perfumer Robert Bienaimé at Houbigant, who had used an aldehyde (C-12 MNA) in the composition of his hugely successful perfume Quelques Fleurs from 1912. Auguste Michel, who had moved from Rallet to Brocard, therefore knew the formula for Bouquet de Napoleon, which became the starting point for the creation of his Le Bouquet Favori de l'Impératrice, or The Empress's Favourite Bouquet. According to Natalya Dolgopolova, this means that in

1912–13, identical – or at least related – perfumes were created in two different Moscow factories under two different names.[23] Ernest Beaux of Rallet & Co. took the formula for Bouquet de Napoleon and Bouquet de Catherine with him to France, where he created Chanel No. 5, while Auguste Michel's career took him from Rallet to Brocard and then, when Brocard was nationalized in 1917, to Novaya Zarya.[24]

In any case, Krasnaya Moskva was released into the world to become the best-known Soviet perfume, and after the demise of the Soviet Union and a brief hiatus resulting from the privatization of the perfume industry, the fragrance returned to the Russian market as a successful remake. The smell of this third-generation Krasnaya Moskva is probably far removed from the original scent. In order to experience that original scent – to actually smell it – you would have to reconstruct the earlier versions using the original formulas and original ingredients. Another possibility would be to find a tightly sealed, well-preserved bottle and open it. Or you could go by descriptions of the scent from Soviet experts such as R. A. Fridman: 'A warm and delicate, even somewhat hot, yet intimate and soft perfume. A typically female perfume.'[25]

If it seems that knowledge was safely transferred and continuity maintained here, it was thanks to yet another coincidence – as revealed in an interview from the 1930s – that Auguste Michel was the man responsible for this continuity. After living through the turmoil of revolution and civil war in Moscow, Michel wanted to return home, following much of the rest of Moscow's French community who had already gone back to France. But the passport he submitted to the authorities in central Moscow to apply for a visa was never given back to him. Even without papers, he was given a residence permit, so he stayed and resumed work at the nationalized Brocard factory. This carried on until diplomatic

3 Brocard bottle

relations were restored between France and the Soviet Union in 1924. Then Michel finally got his passport back. But he opted to stay in Soviet Russia – perhaps because he was able to work again, perhaps because he had found the love of his life there. In any case, there seems to be no doubt that Michel played a significant role in the re-establishment of the Russian perfume industry after the revolution, which itself brought about a 'paradigm shift' in the world of fragrances.

Before the revolution, the highly developed Russian perfume industry had been shaped largely by foreign (mostly French) firms that competed fiercely for the huge Russian–Eurasian market. But after the industry was nationalized, its priorities were radically different. Its main focus then became the mass production of everyday toiletries and cosmetics for the general population. The foreign experts had departed, the supply chains for importing and exporting essential ingredients had been disrupted, and the entire perfume sector had to be reorganized and placed on a new footing.

The factories in the soap and perfume industry were first consolidated under a committee known as Tsentrozhir, or the Main Committee of the Fat Industry of the Supreme Council of the National Economy (VSNKh), and then, from 1921, in a trust referred to as Zhirkost. When the New Economic Policy (NEP) began in the early 1920s, there were around 470 such trusts. All major cosmetics enterprises were incorporated into these trusts, including the former Brocard and Rallet factories. They produced perfumes, soap, eau de cologne, powders and toothpaste, all of which were also given new names. The cosmetics trust, which was reorganized multiple times, has gone down in Soviet history under the French-sounding name TeZhe. This abbreviation stood for Gosudarstvennyy Trest Zhirovoy i Kosti Obrabatyvayushchey Promyshlennosti, or the State Trust of the Fat and Bone Processing Industry. TeZhe (pronounced like a French *tejé*) became a brand name and the quintessential Soviet cosmetics label of the 1920s and 1930s. In 1926–7, TeZhe had 11 factories with 6,120 workers and 652 salaried employees, with perfume accounting for only a small portion of production.[26] With its French-sounding name, TeZhe was in semantic competition with French brands still familiar from the pre-revolutionary period, including Rallet, Coty, Guerlain and Houbigant. It also operated boutiques, some of them quite luxurious, in major Soviet cities, especially in hotels frequented by foreigners. TeZhe covered every sector relevant to perfume production, including chemical labs, glass-cutting factories and retail outlets. In its scope and range of products, the Soviet cosmetics and perfume trust became the largest of its kind in the world.

TeZhe stood for the return of sweet smells after years

of war and civil war, but it also glossed over the reality that the industry was taking an entirely new path. Perfumery was now part of a state enterprise beholden no longer to the laws of supply and demand or the 'anarchical competition' of brands, but instead to an economic plan. The production of perfume thus became a state matter, and deciding on preferred fragrances and cosmetics, perfumes and labels, became the order of the day for the People's Commissar for Food Production and Light Industry. Even the empire of scent was now governed by the 'primacy of politics'.

The scent of a perfume once known as Bouquet de Napoleon or Bouquet de Catherine was the starting point for two other perfumes that were revolutionary in their own way. The scent was (nearly) identical, but it would take two different routes into modernity in the years (and decades) to come. A paradigm shift would take place in design as well – one that would find expression in the appearance of the bottles. Everything moved in the direction of simplicity – in one case, likely as a response to a surfeit of playfulness and ornamental excess; in the other, out of pure necessity. Still, the shapes of the bottles have a touch of geometry, functionalism and Suprematism about them. The labels for the perfumes from Brocard were probably created by an artist named Nikolai Strunnikov, while the packaging and the bottle for Krasnaya Moskva were designed by Andrei Yevseyev. Vladimir Rossinski is another unjustly forgotten artist who had also previously worked for Brocard. Before the revolution, he had designed the tasteful commemorative publication for Brocard's fiftieth anniversary (1864–1914), which recounted the company's history in part through coloured cartoons that were spectacular for their time. TeZhe adopted many aspects of the pre-revolutionary designs.[27] In the period of the New Economic Policy, from around 1921 to 1928, the old designs lived on in a slightly modernized form, but the names of the products changed. One poster advertised a loose powder with the sweet-sounding name Swan Down, while another featured a product named Spartakiade, recalling the proletarian games. Old and new forms coexisted, a situation often found in societies in transition and under a diarchy. But this particular transition would involve a collision in the world of fragrances, and it would not leave the creators of those fragrances untouched.

Scentscapes:
Proust's madeleine and
historiography

A drop of perfume can hold the entire history of the twentieth century. When Gabrielle Coco Chanel met the perfumer Ernest Beaux between the autumn of 1920 and the spring of 1921 in Grasse, the world capital of fragrance on the Riviera, to choose one of his compositions, she had no way of knowing that the formula for the scent that would become internationally famous as Chanel No. 5 was already familiar elsewhere – in Moscow.[1]

Chanel No. 5 and Red Moscow belong to different worlds, but they both represent a departure from the *belle époque* and a revolution in the world of fragrance – even though they both owed their creation to the anniversary of a dynasty destined to fall. We know much about the success of Chanel No. 5, but very little about the importance of Red Moscow. The Chanel No. 5 bottle has a place of honour in the Museum of Modern Art in New York, while the Red Moscow bottle only became an object of desire for vintage collectors at flea markets and antique shops in the late Soviet period, and particularly after the end of the Soviet Union.[2] And Marilyn Monroe's quip that she wore 'a few drops of Chanel No. 5' to bed and nothing else has become not just an advertising slogan but a piece of cultural heritage.

André Malraux believed that France's international image in the twentieth century was shaped by three figures: Picasso, Chanel and de Gaulle. George Bernard Shaw viewed Coco Chanel and Marie Curie as the most important women of the twentieth century.[3] Polina Zhemchuzhina-Molotova, by contrast, is practically unknown. We associate her with her husband Vyacheslav Molotov, who, in turn, is associated with the German–Soviet non-aggression pact of 23 August 1939, or at the very least with the Molotov cocktail (though he could not claim copyright on the term).[4] The stories of these two women follow different trajectories, but they are connected and help us to understand something of the internal workings of an epoch that was more deeply divided than almost any other: the 'Age of Extremes' (Eric Hobsbawm) and the lengthy partition of the world that followed it. To tell these two stories is to tell parallel tales whose protagonists knew almost nothing of one another, or barely took note of one another. Their stories are worth pursuing, even if it seems inappropriate to devote all too much attention to fragrances, scents and luxury in the shifting and groaning framework of a world order grown old in the twenty-first century.[5] But it is really only now, after the end of the epoch that saw the world divided in two, that we can recount the history of these scents, and, though doing so may not give us a key to what happened in the twentieth century, it can at least give us a better understanding of it. Perhaps it is true that the wide world reflected in a drop of water can also be found in a drop of perfume, which reveals something of the aroma of the century for which it was composed.

We need no 'olfactory turn' to explain (much less justify) any scholarly interest that even historians might take in the world of scents and fragrances. Pioneering works such as Alain Corbin's *The Foul and the Fragrant* interpret the world as a world of odours, and consider the history of odours to be integral to understanding historical lifeworlds, thus giving the sense of smell its due in historical scholarship. And Patrick Süskind's *Perfume* is not just a brilliantly constructed crime novel, it also revived awareness of the importance of the sense of smell and ensured that the history of odorous substances, perfume production and the effects of fragrances received the attention they deserve. It should be clear by now that, to perceive the historical world, it is not only the eye and ear that are 'relevant', with their off-hand acceptance of the privilege granted to audio-visual stimuli. Other senses come into play here, too: smell, touch, taste.[6] Although the books by Patrick Süskind and Alain Corbin were published in the 1980s, the sense of smell is only gradually coming into its own in historiography. In the hierarchy of senses, it is at the very bottom. It stands for all that is non-conscious, unconscious, non-rational, irrational, uncontrollable, archaic, dangerous. The Enlightenment banished the sense of smell. 'Today's history comes deodorized' (Roy Porter),[7] and sight is considered 'the most rational of the senses'. 'While smell may have become "inessential" in the world of science, in the fields of humanities and social sciences it has only begun to show its potential to open vast new territories of exploration. At the very least, it has demonstrated its ability to inspire.' To put it plainly, we need to 'sniff around' history more.[8]

In wide swathes of Western intellectual thought, we find a suppression of the sense of smell, but also a persistent rebellion against the hegemony of the 'rational' senses. Hegel feels powerless against the spread of 'pure insight', which he compares to the spread of an odour: 'It is on this account that the communication of pure insight is comparable to a silent expansion or to the *diffusion*, say, of a perfume in the unresisting atmosphere.

It is a penetrating infection which does not make itself noticeable beforehand as something opposed to the indifferent element into which it insinuates itself, and therefore cannot be warded off.'[9]

Kant ranks smell as the most 'dispensable' sense in his anthropology and identifies 'stench' as the background with which a smell contrasts, the only way it makes 'sense':

> Which organic sense is the most ungrateful and also seems to be the most dispensable? The sense of *smell*. It does not pay to cultivate it or refine it at all in order to enjoy; for there are more disgusting objects than pleasant ones (especially in crowded places), and even when we come across something fragrant, the pleasure coming from the sense of smell is always fleeting and transient. – But as a negative condition of well-being, this sense is not unimportant, in order not to breathe in bad air (oven fumes, the stench of swamps and animal carcasses), or also not to need rotten things for nourishment.[10]

Nietzsche, by contrast, says of himself: 'My genius is in my nostrils.'[11] And: 'Tell me, my animals: these higher men, all of them – do they perhaps *smell* bad? O pure smells about me! Only now I know and feel how much I love you, my animals.'[12] The Russian perfumer Konstantin Verigin harks back to Arthur Schopenhauer, who refers to the sense of smell as 'the sense of memory, because it recalls to our mind more directly than anything else the specific impression of an event or an environment, even from the most remote past'.[13] And one of the most ruthless observers of the twentieth century, George Orwell, pinpoints smell as the deepest distinction between the classes: '*The lower classes smell* . . . For no feeling of like or dislike is quite so fundamental as a *physical* feeling.'[14]

We perceive not only with our eyes, our perception not only comprises images, and our memory adheres not only to iconic and emblematic signs. Just as there is a 'noise of time' and every epoch has its own sound, every age has its own scentscape. The generations who grew up in the shadow of the Berlin Wall and the Iron Curtain, whose rites of passage involved border crossings, such as the Friedrichstrasse station between East and West Berlin or the Cheb crossing on the old German–Czech border, will probably always have an olfactory memory of those borders. Even after a long period of enlightenment and distance from the specific smells that usually have negative connotations, even now that the world has been progressively deodorized, we cannot simply catapult ourselves out of the realm of scent. We perceive the world not only with our eyes, but also with our nose. The rhythm of the seasons material-izes not only in shades of lightness and darkness, but in shades of smell – the scent of snow on the air, a fresh spring breeze, the heat of summer weighing down on cities and fields, the mustiness of autumn leaves. Day after day, we traverse zones marked out by smells – the steam rising from coffee in a takeaway paper cup, the grease of a chip shop, the technoid whiff of oil and tar as we glide down an escalator into a subway station. We ride in buses where, depending on the temperature and time of year, the perspiration of bodies pressed close can prove stronger than the deodorized layer in which we swathe ourselves each day. We inhale the sharp, almost fruity aroma of petrol at service stations and the generic smell of department stores and supermarkets, where all the differences between an endless variety of goods have melded into a stew of odours difficult to describe.

The slightest disruption to our everyday smells – uncollected rubbish, for instance – pops the deodorized bubble in which we usually live, causes irritation and unease. We must make an effort to bear a stench. We suffer not only from the tyranny of intimacy, but from the world of smells produced by that intimacy. We do not want it to touch us. Progress is measured by the suppression of stench, and what we consider pleasant or repugnant is an aspect of the lordship–bondage relationship described by Hegel and Marx: the struggle between the centre and the periphery, between above and below, between people living in close proximity, between the West and the non-European world. The spread of the 'sanitary convenience' is as reliable an indicator of civilization as the establishment of a parliamentary order – at least according to Somerset Maugham.[15] The smell of progress in the industrial age, the belching smokestacks and chimneys, has been followed by an odourless post-industrial digital economy, and even the creation of smoke-free zones in restaurants to guarantee a pleasant dining experience. In the language of political agitation, the *ancien régime* lands on the 'trash heap of history', and the new era dawns like a paradise with its attendant paradisiacal fragrances.

Literature is full of smells: the scent of flowers, the 'smoke of the fatherland' (Fyodor Tyutchev), the pungency of Soviet Belomorkanal cigarettes. The catastrophes of the twentieth century involved not only apocalyptic landscapes but also the gas of the gas chambers, the stench of the smoke rising from the crematoria, the stink of the camps in which people were left to rot away while still alive. Smells and scents have their own production time and their own expiry time. Smells linger long after regimes have fallen and ideologies have faded – and vice versa. Cycles of scents do not coincide with legislative periods. They live by their own time. Scents can survive revolutions.

The 'scent of the big wide world', as one cigarette brand billed itself, was once associated with the horizons opened up by Pan American Airways. Generations are divided not only by their changing tastes but by their signature scents. Wars create a din and also generate smells of gun smoke, burning and corpses. The air that follows a thunderstorm is fresh, cleansed. We cannot describe the most banal aspects of present or past without mentioning times and places, but nor can we avoid mentioning tastes and smells. We need not debate which of the senses is given priority: sight, sound, touch, smell, taste. Images impress themselves on our memory, but smells take hold there as well. It requires no more than a breath of air and the hint of a scent to bring whole scenes to life in our mind: the waxy smell of a parquet floor, a school stairwell, the aroma of a stationery shop, a gymnasium, incense billowing from a censer during Holy Mass, the smell of petrol from a car – be it an Eastern Trabant or Western Ford.

The odour of an age clings to all phases of life, and it cannot be wrong to take this into account when reconstructing the past. The 'ur-scene' in this process must be the madeleine episode in Marcel Proust's *In Search of Lost Time*, in which a small cake dipped in a cup of tea triggers an 'all-powerful joy' as soon as it touches the narrator's lips. Proust's description of the sense of taste must surely also apply to the sense of smell: 'No sooner had the warm liquid mixed with the crumbs touched my palate than a shiver ran through me and I stopped, intent upon the extraordinary thing that was happening to me. An exquisite pleasure had invaded my senses, something isolated, detached, with no suggestion of its origin.' What follows is several pages of reflection on what had been unleashed by that sensation of taste. There is no logical conclusion, only 'evidence of its felicity':

> Undoubtedly what is thus palpitating in the depths of my being must be the image, the visual memory which, being linked to that taste, is trying to follow it into my conscious mind. But its struggles are too far off, too confused and chaotic; scarcely can I perceive the neutral glow into which the elusive whirling medley of

stirred-up colours is fused, and I cannot distinguish its form, cannot invite it, as the one possible interpreter, to translate for me the evidence of its contemporary, its inseparable paramour, the taste, cannot ask it to inform me what special circumstance is in question, from what period in my past life. . . . And suddenly the memory revealed itself.

The memory is of a specific place, a specific day, a specific scene:

> But when from a long-distant past nothing subsists, after the people are dead, after the things are broken and scattered, taste and smell alone, more fragile but more enduring, more immaterial, more persistent, more faithful, remain poised a long time, like souls, remembering, waiting, hoping, amid the ruins of all the rest; and bear unflinchingly, in the tiny and almost impalpable drop of their essence, the vast structure of recollection.

Everything comes flooding back, the water lilies, the people of the village, their little houses, the church, all of Combray and its environs, all of it 'taking shape and solidity, sprang into being, town and gardens alike, from my cup of tea'.[16]

If this holds true, then the history of perfume and the luxury goods industry is not just a subset of social reality. A drop of perfume is time captured in scent, and the bottle is the vessel that holds the fragrance of time. The fascination with perfume bottles currently in evidence in post-Soviet Russia and elsewhere is more than just a quirk, it is its own 'search for lost time'. The post-Soviet Proust is probably already on the prowl.

The difficulty of actualizing a past scentscape is obvious. The eye can fix on images that have been drawn, documented and reproduced – infinitely rich and differentiated, multi-faceted visual worlds. The ear has access to musical scores, recordings of the aural fabric of a city, the burst of a fanfare before a mass march, the voice from an interview, the speech on an important occasion. Noises and soundscapes can be recorded, retrieved, read, reproduced – everything from chiming bells to loudspeakers. Instruments can be recreated. But even with the most refined biochemical analyses now available to us, where do we stand when it comes to smell as a source of information that is supposed to be reliable, 'intersubjectively reviewable' and 'objective'? Materials have their smell, flowers have their fragrance. In the chemical age, scents can be generated and reproduced at will. But they do not last forever. There is no archive of aromas in which odours can be stored for all eternity and retrieved again. Scents evaporate. They can be described, but for all the richness of language, the description of a scent comes nowhere near the experience of perceiving the infinite nuances of an aroma through the sense of smell, and certainly not through the professionally trained sense of an expert. Attempts to pin down the 'pitches', nuances, voices and spheres of scents in perfumer's organs and written compositions, to objectify them and make them 'readable', are no more than approximations and aids for the novice.

It is no coincidence that histories of fragrances tend to focus on the vessels that hold them, the bottles that continue to exist long after the last traces of the volatile oils and essences have evaporated. They give form to the olfactory composition. The bottles become symbols that are synonymous with the scents they contain. This is why wherever you find bottles, you will find perfume archaeologists: in antique shops, on the many websites run by vintage communities, and in the fragrance categories on eBay. Many cities already have perfume museums, including Paris, Versailles, Grasse, Barcelona, Cologne, Saint Petersburg and Moscow. Much more material will come to light as collectors crawl around in attics and discover bottles of precious exotic scents carefully preserved by grandmothers despite the greatest hardships – the flotsam of past epochs. Amongst all the exhibitions and archives of scents, a special place would have to be reserved for a museum of smells featuring the jars in which the Stasi in East Germany stored scent samples from dissidents, which they used to train and drill their sniffer dogs.

The book at hand will have to make do with the capabilities of a historian who is aware of his limitations, has no laboratory of scents at his disposal and did not train as a perfumer. What he does have, however, is a notion that there is not just a 'noise of time' (Ossip Mandelstam) but also a 'smell of time' – that we move not just through soundscapes, but through scentscapes. If we want to take our leave of the twentieth century, we should do it with all of our senses. We can follow the traces of Chanel No. 5 and Red Moscow as we do so. Let us go back to their mutual starting point, their pre-history. We will track down the authors of the fragrances, who generally do not appear on the labels on the bottles. We will see how history diverges and realize that we are always dealing with more than just a vial of a precious essence – we are dealing with the world concentrated within it. And we will see that what befell the creators of these fragrances in the course of the twentieth century was both asymmetrical and unjust.

When 'the weakest link breaks in the imperialist chain' (Lenin): the world of scents and the olfactory revolution

The careers of the perfumers Ernest Beaux and Auguste Michel were not unique in the period now referred to as the 'first age of globalization'. Moving from companies on the Côte d'Azur to Saint Petersburg or Moscow, founding factories in the new centres of industrialization in Imperial Russia, the emergence of communities of foreigners in the rapidly growing cities of the tsarist empire – none of this was any more exceptional than the flow of traffic that had started in the other direction as well, westwards. Thanks to the Nord Express train service, shuttling between Saint Petersburg and Paris had become routine. Russian butter was shipped to Western Europe, fresh strawberries and flowers from the Riviera were sent north for receptions at the Russian imperial court.

The life trajectories of Beaux and Michel were symptomatic of a world in upheaval. Viktor Lobkovich, a perfume-bottle collector who has unearthed the history of Russian perfume, calls the period from 1821 to 1921[1] the 'golden age of Russian perfumery and cosmetics'.[1] And there is a good deal of evidence that, shortly before the outbreak of World War I, Russia had become a world power not only in the realm of culture but also in the production of cosmetics and perfumes. What factors came together here? First, there was the immense wealth of the Russian aristocracy concentrated in the two capital cities, which were a world away from the backwardness and poverty gripping the rest of the vast country. And then there was the economic revival set in motion by the Great Reforms of the 1860s, which saw Russia become a rapidly developing industrial power in just a few decades, with growth rates that prompted even Trotsky and Lenin to sing the praises of the revolutionary energy of the bourgeoisie. This led to the emergence of a small but relatively prosperous middle class with money to spend, who could afford products previously considered luxury goods reserved only for a tiny circle of aristocrats.[2] In the largest country on earth by landmass (with the exception of the British Empire and the colonial empire of France at the time), a huge market had emerged, extending from Lodz to Vladivostok and Helsinki to Tashkent and beyond – to China, Japan and Persia.

All of this was reflected in the bottles and their labels, the names of the fragrances and soaps that became trademarks throughout the empire, and the posters advertising the industry's products, and it all generated a shared concept of upscale consumption that increasingly spilled over to the general population, which was interested mainly in everyday toiletries such as soap, powder and eau de cologne. The illustrated books published by collectors such as Viktor Lobkovich, Veniamin Kozharinov and Natalya Dolgopolova are a testament to their authors' fascination with the aesthetic richness, colour and ingenuity of the designs of the time. And these designs, in turn, reveal the extent to which the designers participated in the aesthetic revolution of the Russian 'Silver Age'.[3] Works by the masters of the

Russian Art Nouveau – Mikhail Vrubel, Ivan Bilibin, Konstantin Somov – flowed from salons and galleries into the newly established department stores, hotels and fashion boutiques.[4]

In the market for perfumes and colognes, Russia was certainly not a 'blank sheet' on which French perfumers were the first to make their mark. Like every other country, Russia had its own culture of scent – one shaped by the natural world, flora and fauna, the country's unique climatic conditions with its long winters breaking into early spring storms, its resin-drenched forests and the sub-tropical gardens on the Black Sea coast. It had always had its own traditions, its cloister gardens with medicinal plants and its spices imported via the Silk Road, not least frankincense and myrrh, their smoke pluming into the domes of Orthodox churches during services.[5] The pioneers in the perfume and cosmetics industry of tsarist Russia included Russian entrepreneurs. But the birth of industrialization and development of a domestic market in the nineteenth century brought about something new. Foreign businessmen began to settle in Russia and establish companies that would go on to win the *Grand Prix* in 1900 at the International Exposition in Paris, the Mecca of fragrances. Brocard & Co. and Rallet & Co. were just two of many examples.[6]

In 1832, for instance, Prussian-born Karl Ivanovich Ferrein bought a pharmacy on Nikolskaya Street in the centre of Moscow. Decades later it had become one of the largest operations of its kind, with its own chemical–pharmaceutical labs, a chemical factory, plantations of medicinal herbs, and a workshop for manufacturing apothecary jars. In 1896, it received the gold medal at the All-Russian Industrial and Art Exhibition in Nizhny Novgorod. By 1914, it had more than 1,000 employees, including 3 pharmacists with science degrees and over 100 with medical training. On the eve of World War I, the pharmacy was issuing around 3,000 prescriptions every day. After the revolution, it became the headquarters of the Soviet Pharmacy Administration.[7]

Roman Romanovich Köhler (Keler in Russian) opened a chemical–pharmaceutical factory in 1862. Soon afterwards, he established several facilities for manufacturing essential oils, thus cutting the price of these expensive essences. His factories produced the tannin that was urgently needed by the Russian textile industry to pit itself against foreign competitors in the domestic market. By 1900, the Köhler company had a plant in Moscow that made glass for apothecaries, confectioners and perfumeries. It also ran factories in the surrounding region for producing acids, essential oils, and toilet, medical and ordinary soaps, and it had branches in every major city from central Russia to the Far East. The eau de toilette made by 'R. Köhler & Co.' was advertised on opulent posters. Its products were sold not only in Russia, but in Bukhara, Khiva, Persia, China. The company made mobile pharmaceutical chests as well – medicine cabinets for the home, first-aid kits for travel – which could be found in the most remote provincial towns.

The first perfume factory in Moscow opened in 1843, founded by the Frenchman Alphonse Antonovich Rallet, with forty employees and one steam engine. Rallet imported raw materials from France, hired foreign specialists and planted fields of the essential oil crops needed by the perfume industry – a novelty in Russia at the time. Products made by Rallet were exported to France, Germany, Turkey and the Balkans. Rallet became the purveyor to His Imperial Majesty the Emperor of All the Russias, as well as to the King of Romania, the Shah of Persia and the Prince of Montenegro. Branches opened in Yekaterinburg, Tashkent, Tbilisi, Kharkov, Irkutsk and Vilnius. In 1899, the company built a state-of-the-art factory in

Moscow's Butyrsky district, which soon received the highest accolades at every major industrial exhibition. After the revolution, Rallet & Co. was nationalized and renamed State Soap Factory No. 4, and its perfume production all but stopped. In 1922 it was renamed again, this time becoming the State Soap and Cosmetics Factory Svoboda.[8] It was at Rallet and Co. that the Moscow-born, French-trained Ernest Beaux had begun his career in 1902, under the guidance of head perfumer Alexandre Lemercier – and it was here that he developed his Bouquet de Napoleon in 1912.

But the most iconic Russian perfumery was the company founded by Henri Afanasyevich Brocard, who was born into a French perfumer's family in 1838. His father had owned a perfume factory in France but left it behind to set up a new one in Philadelphia. When Brocard's father returned to Paris, the American factory was run by his sons. In 1861, Henri Brocard took his father's advice and travelled to Russia, where he worked as a lab assistant in a perfume factory. He later became self-employed and then founded his own company in 1864, in a former stable with primitive equipment. He achieved success with his soaps – children's soap, honey soap, amber soap – in part because each piece of children's soap had a letter of the Russian alphabet printed on it, and the label for the 'People's Pomade' featured short fables by Ivan Krylov. Brocard thus gave even the poorer classes access to soap (the cheapest type, the 'people's soap' known as Narodnoe, cost 1 kopeck per piece), as well as an opportunity to learn the alphabet. The house of Brocard was responsible for other novelties as well, including the first transparent glycerine soap in Russia, pieces of soap shaped like cucumbers, and an eau de cologne for mass consumption.

Brocard opened sumptuous boutiques, the largest of which was in the brand-new trading rows on Red Square (which would later become GUM department store), and the company expanded its range and created new scents. The shops were run by Brocard's wife, Charlotte, a Belgian whose outstanding command of Russian made her a leading figure in Moscow society. The successful businessman was also a collector and patron of the arts, with his own exhibition rooms filled with paintings, porcelain, tapestries and valuable furniture, the opening of which attracted all of Moscow society. By the time Brocard died in 1900, his products had scooped up awards at nearly every world expo in Paris, Brussels, Chicago and Barcelona. For its 50th jubilee, the company published a luxurious book with outstanding typography and illustrations, a testament to the 'Brocard Empire' that would produce Bouquet de Catherine to commemorate the 300th anniversary of the Romanov dynasty. Brocard was also nationalized after the revolution, and under the name Novaya Zarya it formed the core of the Soviet perfume and cosmetics industry. Its most popular product would be Krasnaya Moskva.[9]

This list of companies should include the one owned by Adolphe Siou, which was the first confectionery firm in Russia to produce chocolate, but which also made perfume. Its new, ultra-modern plant was renamed Bolshevik after the revolution and became the largest and most important factory for pastries and sweets, operating right to the end of the Soviet Union. By 1913, just before the war, Moscow counted a total of eighteen perfume manufacturers and sixty-three businesses specializing in perfume.[10]

The perfume industry's impressive boom in the Russian Empire was driven in part by Russian perfumers, including Alexander Mitrofanovich Ostroumov, who invented an anti-dandruff soap that met with great success, as well as a cream named Metamorphosa for treating rashes and freckles. Ostroumov founded the Russian cosmetology industry and had laboratories and branch offices in Saint Petersburg, Odessa, Tashkent and Warsaw. He was also an innovative advertiser who featured famous actresses and ballerinas on his posters, thus bolstering the seduction of scent with the seduction of images. The S. I. Chepelevetsky and Sons perfume co-operative also achieved fame beyond the borders of Russia, winning awards at exhibitions in Milan, Paris, Madrid and The Hague.[11]

New importance was accorded to posters, packaging and bottle designs, which emphasized the exotic and precious nature of the fragrances. Packaging was no longer a secondary concern – it was a fight for attention. Advertising was viewed as an art, and it took inspiration from the renowned painters and graphic designers of the Silver Age. This was the era of Art Nouveau, and the style found its way into public and private spaces around 1900 in the form of cosmetics and perfumes, which carried both the scent of the new age and its aesthetic tastes to the farthest reaches of Russia and beyond. The bottles, cases, boxes and gift sets of the time are a record of the predilections of Imperial Russia, which remained alive long after 1917. The perfume names – Carmen, My Babushka's Bouquet, Renommé, Extraits de Fleurs, First Love's Kiss – lodged in the memory of generations of Russians. The labels on the bottles subsequently produced by the Red Dawn factory still boasted the names of once-legendary companies, reminding consumers that the respective perfumeries were 'formerly Brocard' or 'formerly Rallet'. The miniature artworks made of cut crystal, with ornate stoppers and gold-framed labels often bearing the signet of the double-headed eagle – indicating that the company was a purveyor to the imperial court – held fragrances called Lily-of-the-Valley Extrait, Delicieux Rococo, White Heliotrope and Bouquet de Napoleon (showing Napoleon with the characteristic strands of hair across his brow). Metal powder compacts in silk-lined cases bore names like White Musk, Swan Feather, Hungarian Pomade. But after 1917, the toilet soap would be renamed 'October', a product of Factory No. 5, whose logo featured not only the hammer and sickle but also a worker in an apron slaying the dragon of capitalist exploitation.

The posters, perfume bottles and powder compacts, the prizes awarded at industrial exhibitions, the names of the cities in which the companies were based – taken together, they give an impression of the scent of the empire, and they delineate a topography of the empire of scents from the first age of globalization.[12]

This empire of scents was surveyed by a perfumer who, with a trained and unerring sense of smell, immersed himself once again in that fallen realm. The man who took the measure of Imperial Russia with his nose was named Konstantin Mikhailovich Verigin (1899–1982), and 'Fragrance' was the Russian title of his memoirs, written in the 1960s in Paris and published in the same city in 1965.[13]

What does a perfumer do? Alla Belfer, one of the most experienced perfumers in the Soviet Union, described this highly specialized profession as follows:

A perfumer must not only be familiar with a colossal number of smells, he must also know how one smell harmonises with others, which composition will preserve its aroma on the skin, and how it will work as the smell of a soap or in a lotion or in other cosmetics. . . . Over the course of many years of work, it becomes fairly easy for the perfumer to write a formula for a perfume, and he can sense it! There is a peculiar inner 'nose' (*nyukh*) for smells, but this is only perfected through a very great deal of experience . . . It is much like how a composer composes. He writes notes on paper, but he hears the music in his head. Our teachers once taught us to compose chords of 2, 3, 4 scents and remember how they smelled in various compositions. It takes many years to learn that. After completing training, you must

4 Konstantin Verigin, 1940

spend ten more years working on the delicate science of scent composition to become a proper composer of fragrances.[14]

Mikhail Loskutov put it similarly in his essay on Auguste Michel:

A perfume bottle is like a choir or an orchestra, Master Michel says. There are gentle voices, violoncellos, there are violins. And there are basses. These are thunderous smells. Taken on its own, such a bass smell would be unbearable. But here they all blend together. You hear them all only in harmony. You do not perceive them separately. And you are not supposed to.

Michel goes on to say:

Oh, I know full well that composing perfumes does not mean simply pouring a series of pleasant-smelling liquids into a glass. You also need unpleasant and neutral smells, fixators, amplifiers. For different compositions you need different doses, substances, production conditions. . . . You must have a knowledge of botany, chemistry, perfumery, many years in the noble profession of the perfumer.

And Alexei Pogudkin, creator of the perfume Rusalka, is said to have repeatedly listened to Antonín Dvořák's opera of the same name. Fragrances are not created by chance; they take time.[15]

Verigin's book is, first and foremost, a survey of pre-revolutionary Russia as a landscape of scents. He confirms that smell is probably the most intensive sense when it comes to remembrance and reminiscence, a space of memory untethered from the fixation on sights and sounds. Verigin makes explicit reference to Arthur Schopenhauer. With forty years distance, he looks back on his childhood and youth spent in Yalta on the Crimean Peninsula and then at various family seats in the central Russian Oryol Oblast, in the Bashkir city of Ufa, in Simbirsk on the Volga, and back in Saint Petersburg, where he had been born in 1899 to an extremely wealthy noble family. He served in the military in World War I and then joined the White Army after the revolution. When it was defeated, he fled via Constantinople, and Panchevo in Serbia, to France, where he studied chemistry at Lille Catholic University and then worked in a perfume factory. It was there, in 1926, that his aristocratic family connections brought him into contact with Ernest Beaux, who enticed him to work for Bourjois and

Chanel. Verigin admired – and, indeed, revered – Beaux and remained close to him for over thirty years, until Beaux's death on 9 June 1961. Verigin's 'memoirs of a perfumer' are largely also an homage to the pioneer he so adored. Verigin was involved in the composition of a number of Beaux's famous perfumes, including Soir de Paris (1926), Bois des Îles (1929) and Cuir de Russie (1935). During World War II, Verigin was put to work as a forced labourer in a chemical plant in Munich, but he returned to Paris after the war to resume working for Chanel.[16]

The second part of Verigin's memoirs describes the entire complex process of perfume production in detail, from composing a perfume and locking away the formula in a safe, through various extraction methods and the acquisition of raw materials, to the design, advertising and marketing. It also offers an in-depth characterization of the personality and achievements of Ernest Beaux. But the first and most important part of his book is dedicated to the universe of scents in the Russian Empire, which Verigin was forced to leave for good after the defeat in the Civil War. It is also a 'search for lost time', very much in the spirit of Marcel Proust, but written in the language of a trained chemist and perfumer. One could read this section of his book as a proper exercitation, a methodical perusal of the scentscape of his childhood and youth in Russia, written not just as an étude but with systematic intent – the account of an individual who returns to roam, explore and survey a past world with the trained senses of a professional. Each section is preceded by a few lines of poetry – by Afanasy Fet and Nikolai Gumilev, Alexander Pushkin and Ivan Bunin – which speak to the sense of smell or a remembered scent or fragrance. In keeping with Hans J. Rindisbacher's study *The Smell of Books*, these writers are invoked as key witnesses for the formative power and evident nature of the olfactory experience.[17]

Every landscape and climate that Verigin was exposed to and experienced is accounted for here, from Crimea to Oryol Oblast. Every period of his life is brought to mind once more: the spacious house with its suites of rooms, the country estate, the city. He traverses the spaces of his childhood once again: the scent of coffee in the morning, the wolf pelt in front of the bed, the aroma of expensive cigarettes, the smell of furniture used again after a long winter. Sounds are accompanied by smells. It is in his Aunt Lelya's boudoir that the author, inspired by the scent of perfume, chooses his future profession early on. A stationery shop smells of cedar pencils, the chemical odour of bottled ink, the metallic tang of quill pens, the leather of his school satchel and the belt that holds his jacket closed. The initial sensations that would shape his entire life are associated with smells. 'Those first impressions, first sympathies and friendships so often proved to be decisive to one's whole life.'[18] Every time and every place has its odour: the start of the school year with the smell of the school hallway, the smell of mushrooms in summer. Christmas, Easter and Lent are each tied to the memory of a specific smell. The landscapes of the Russian Empire are assembled into a landscape of scents: the promenade and beach in Yalta; the wide fields of Oryol Oblast; the fresh, cold air of a snowy Russian day. Verigin quotes the Russian émigré poet Don-Aminado:

> But there is one smell in the world
> And there is one delight in the world
> It is a Russian winter afternoon
> It is the Russian smell of snow.[19]

Konstantin Verigin follows his nose through the 'little world' of his childhood home: his father's study, the dining room, his mother's rooms, even the neighbours are characterized by 'how their house smells' – it 'smells of order', a smell that includes whole bouquets of flowers in vases with their different aromas, violets, lavender, hyacinth, lilacs, roses, wisteria, magnolia, acacia, jasmine, carnations, reseda, vanilla-scented heliotrope. In his mind's eye, he sees the bottles on the dressing table, the small crystal boxes with silver closures that the children were forbidden to touch, holding exquisite substances to be dusted onto clothing and furs or dabbed on the skin before his mother donned her grand hat with white ostrich feathers and kissed the children goodbye.[20] He even remembers the brands found in wealthy households at the time: Vera Violetta, Roger & Gallet, Coeur de Jeannette, Rose de France, Quelques Fleurs by Houbigant, L'Origan, La Rose Jacqueminot and Jasmin de Corse by Coty, Rue de la Paix by Guerlain and a few English perfumes he can no longer recall.

This is the scent of an entire culture, and this culture – particularly when viewed from the perspective of loss – is depicted as an idyllic world in which (as the Russian reviewer Olga Kushlina rightly criticizes) the reek of carbolic and kerosene, the sharp smell of makhorka, vomit and blood, the stench that rises from the bowels of a deeply divided and unjust world simply do not exist. While Russia subsisted on bitter brine, Verigin indulges in memories of the smell of the oak flooring in his family's stately home in Saint Petersburg, the paradisiacal scent of lily-of-the-valley on the estate in Oryol, and he immerses himself once more in the 'symphony of luxurious aromas' in his family's residence at 16 Nikolaevskaya Street in Yalta, which he was forced to flee hastily and forever on 2 November 1920, embarking on a ship to Constantinople while bells pealed and the tsarist anthem was played.[21] Kushlina accuses Verigin of 'odour fanaticism' and 'scent mysticism' because he equates the pleasant smells of the aristocratic Russia of his family with the olfactory world of the tsarist empire itself and, moreover, ignores or even negates the infernally fetid haunts of the 'humiliated and insulted'.[22]

Indeed, even war, revolution and civil war have an olfactory dimension – and what truly astounds is that it has taken so long to acknowledge the elemental experience of the smell of a collapsing world. That said, Alain Corbin produced an exemplary study of the dissolution and collapse of the olfactory world of the *ancien régime* in France, and comparable studies of Russia have now begun to follow.[23]

On the centenary of the Russian Revolution, the German historian Jan Plamper ventured to recount the story of this radical upheaval as a story of the senses. In Plamper's telling, this history – which has been analysed for so long as a battle of ideas, clash of factions, and series of strategic debates and tactical manoeuvres – starts to change on the quiet. John Reed's classic *Ten Days That Shook the World* becomes a 'sense scape' and 'sensory-mental topography of the city', documenting a 'sensory pandemonium' in which the melody of the 'Marseillaise' and singing of the 'Internationale' play as important a role as the noise of street fighting and the odour that drifts across the city from the burning district court and its smouldering stacks of files. Transitions from one 'stage' of the Russian Revolution to the next, and degrees of acceleration and radicalization, are acoustically marked by the transition from the tsarist anthem to the 'Internationale', but they can also be discerned in the eruption of an 'olfactory class struggle'.[24] The aroma of the exquisite cigars still being savoured in bourgeois salons becomes the symbol of a world unravelling at the seams. The senses adapt to the loss of familiar smells as supplies of firewood dwindle and bakeries no longer turn out loaves of white French bread.

Class consciousness develops an olfactory dimension here, as officials, employees and society ladies are forced to come to terms with an altered and increasingly fragmented world of odours. Overnight, their comfortable world is penetrated by different sounds, different smells. Streetcars (those that are still running) are now crowded with soldiers and deserters streaming back from the front line, bringing with them the odour of men who have not bathed for weeks in the field. The world of the perfumed young women who stroll Nevsky Prospekt in Petrograd or Tverskaya Street in Moscow now collides with the sharp smell of hand-rolled papirosa cigarettes. Theatre performances are no longer reserved for an exclusive and educated audience which has internalized the rules of such events, with their intervals, applause and moments of silence. Now the red velvet and chandelier-bedecked halls are overrun by people who never had a chance to see a performance before and who act accordingly: smoking, spitting sunflower seeds on the shiny tiles in the foyer and generally misbehaving. The odour of the front lines and the bivouac, the sweat of factory work, the stench of overcrowded train carriages – it all forces its way into the perfumed and deodorized realm of high culture, bringing new sounds and new smells perceived by the usual bourgeois and aristocratic audiences as being unpleasant, uncultivated, repellent, repugnant – indeed, barbaric.

These initial advances merely breached the walls of the hermetically sealed and orderly olfactory world of the *ancien régime*, but this whole world would soon break apart into islands, enclaves, an archipelago, isolated havens of sweet smells. And the moment its olfactory world was called into question, 'society' realized that everything it had once taken for granted was gone: the salons, the festive soirées, the inner realm of the bourgeoisie and aristocracy, the interior of a world destined to fall, complete with the scents and aromas that impregnated it. The social revolution targeted the innermost part of this world, the homes that once sheltered the propertied classes, where they settled and lived out their lives, which were now invaded by 'newcomers' following the call of the 'Internationale':

Make a clean slate of the past!
Enslaved masses, arise, arise!
The world's foundation will change
We are nothing, let us be everything!

In bourgeois dwellings that previously housed a single family and their domestic staff, each one of the eight rooms was now occupied by an entire family; instead of six or eight people living in a house, there would be up to forty. A lifeworld was transformed here, not just for a brief moment but for many years, indeed decades – and not just for a single family but for generations of city-dwellers. The birth of the *kommunalka*, or communal apartment, from the collapse of the old order; the flight of the rural peasantry to the factories and the cities; the regime of intimacy that inevitably emerged from the enforced, involuntary cohabitation of total strangers thrown together – this would be the stuff of the everyday drama of the coexistence of millions of Soviet citizens in the decades to come, right to the end of the Soviet Union. And there was an 'olfactory dimension' to this, one which has been described often and is easy to imagine.[25]

The revolutionary regime did not just accept the 'olfactory revolution' as an unavoidable side-effect of social upheaval, it explicitly encouraged it by formulating a new code, so to speak, for the olfactory world of the new society. Just as the new state power had a specific jargon (Stephen Kotkin refers to it as 'speaking Bolshevik'[26]) and specific behaviours, it wanted a specific world of smell appropriate to the New Soviet Man and New Soviet Woman, one in which all forms of refinement and fragrance were repudiated as expressions of softness, and even decadence, and perfume was branded the very epitome of a bourgeois lifestyle. From this point on, the smells of the world of work – primarily meaning physical labour associated with exertion, sweat and grime – were in conflict with the scents of idleness, coddling, decadence. Perfumes could be as revealing as the tell-tale eyeglasses of the bourgeois intellectual or the 'white hands' that identified an aristocratic lady or member of the intelligentsia. For a while, at least, perfumes became as much of a class characteristic as attire that was not in keeping with the work clothes of the young communist or the leather overcoat of the functionary. The intimate connection between fashion and perfume is also apparent here, because just as the revolutionary class had a scent, the revolutionary proletariat had a dress code.

Worlds of scent were in conflict here. In the transitional phase between the dissolution of the old world and creation of a new one, olfactory realms overlapped in something like a representation of the continued existence of class antagonism. Verigin even writes of the 'smell of the dying classes' and the 'smell of the new society'. Sweet smells disappeared from the centre of power, making way for the rise of the periphery, the previously marginalized. Looking back, Verigin summarizes his feelings: 'For the Russian nobility, the new age brought the odour of death with it. The oppressive smell of corpses and sweetish smell of blood became the olfactory space in which the Russian nobility now existed.' Conversely, the smell now clinging to the representatives of power, the state and party functionaries, was that of leather coats and cars – the outfits and status symbols of revolutionary society. The overthrown class was humiliated by being forced to do the dirty jobs previously handled by the lower classes: 'bourgeois elements' were assigned to shovel snow, clean toilets and collect rubbish.

The time of the New Economic Policy between 1921 and 1928 was just such a transitional period. On the black market you could still find the remainders of old soaps and perfumes, and the fine women of the elite – Larissa Reissner, Alexandra Kollontai, Nina Berberova – daubed themselves with fragrances of Parisian and pre-revolutionary provenance (the Bolshevik aristocrat Alexandra Kollontai, who served as a diplomatic envoy in a series of different countries, was fond of Soir de Paris from Bourjois). The travellers, diplomats, journalists and writers who were able to journey westwards to capitalist countries with their 'red passports' returned from their trips abroad with soaps, perfumes and highly coveted fashion magazines such as *Harper's Bazaar* and *Vogue*; the connections here had not yet been completely severed. Echoes of the past reverberated in the names of cosmetics as well. Many perfumes in the 1920s still went by names such as Bouquet, Aroma of Love, Spring Flowers, Ambrosia, White Rose, Tatiana's Bouquet, Valeriya's Caprice, Tea Rose, Rosebud, Ai-Petri (a mountain peak in Crimea), Mary Pickford and Floria.

The names of the new era were political; the olfactory world was semantically bolshevized. Perfumes and cosmetics were now called Golden Grain, New Life (Novyy Byt), Red Poppy (Krasnyy Mak), Red Moscow (Krasnaya Moskva), Spartakiada, Hero of the North (Geroy Severa), Avantgarde. Later yet, in the *Sturm und Drang* of the First Five-Year Plan, they would bear the names of the building blocks of communism: Stratostat (a stratospheric balloon), On Watch, Our Answer to Collective Farmers (Nash Otvet Kolkhoznikam), Pioneer, Tank, White Sea Canal (Belomorsky Kanal), Hello to the Chelyuskin Crew (Privyet Chelyuskinam, named after a Soviet expeditionary ship that got trapped in the Arctic pack ice in 1933, though the crew was rescued), Collective Farm Victory (Kolkhoznaya Pobeda).

And the new scents became a trademark of the new class of social climbers.

In communal apartments, the smell from the shared kitchen, the smell of cabbage soup, overlapped with the pleasant aromas that the 'former people' who had found accommodation there could not do without. The antagonism between grime and cleanliness, fragrance and stench, also penetrated the political sphere and made itself known whenever there was talk of the 'crystalline purity of the party', the 'festering bourgeois intelligentsia' or 'cleansing'. The scent of lavender referenced in the *chansons* of Alexander Vertinsky represented decline, decadence and degeneracy in the eyes of the guardians of Bolshevik morality. Political opponents were soon branded 'Trotskyist–Pyatakovist degenerates' who belonged on the 'dung heap' or 'rubbish heap of history'.[27]

When the perfume and cosmetics industry was reorganized at the end of the Civil War, the focus of the sector changed as well. The industry's revival was an important step towards normalization after a decade of fighting, with millions dead, wounded or displaced. The Soviet government revived some pre-revolutionary traditions (reluctantly at first) and then tried to outdo them by offering soaps for mass consumption, and perfumes such as Red Moscow in place of The Empress's Favourite Bouquet. But one key factor was necessary before perfume as a symbol of high culture could be rehabilitated and a genuinely Soviet fragrance could be developed: there needed to be a class of people who, unlike the masses, could voice and realize their aspirations for a better, more beautiful life. This was the 'New Class' (Milovan Djilas) of the 1930s that emerged from the upheaval of collectivization, industrialization and Stalin's purges.[28] Producing specifically Soviet fragrances became the focus of the perfume industry, whose development and modernization followed the rhythm of the Five-Year Plans. The industry's embrace of clear, concise, abstract forms brought it into alignment with the forms pioneered in the West by the Chanel No. 5 bottle – an indication that there were two paths within modernity.

The metamorphosis of the perfume bottle in post-revolutionary Russia, and the turn towards simple, clean shapes, was paralleled by Coco Chanel's decision to present Chanel No. 5 in a square of glass. Chanel's biographer Edmonde Charles-Roux described the bottle's design as follows:

> The Chanel container absolutely contradicted the convoluted presentations favored by its rivals – the cupid-shaped flasks and lace- or flower-etched urns – because the other perfume makers still believed that such affectations were an effective sales device. The noteworthy feature of the sharp-cornered cube Gabrielle put on the market was that it transferred the imagination to a different dimension. It was no longer the container that aroused desire, but its contents. It was no longer the object that decided the sales; the emphasis shifted to the one faculty really concerned: the sense of smell, brought into confrontation with this golden fluid imprisoned in a crystal cube and made visible solely in order to be desired. Much might also be said of the trim graphics of the label, which rendered obsolete all the curves and curlicues adorning perfumes of the past; and of the stark harmony of this presentation which relied solely on the contrast of black and white – black, black forever; and of the title, lastly, composed of the single word 'Chanel' joined to one dry number and tossed into shop windows like a tip; 'Play the five.'[29]

The new design disavowed and discredited everything that had gone before as being outmoded and obsolete. A closer look reveals that this was not just a chance artistic inspiration, it was the aesthetic form of a departure from an age that had run its course. It was no different with the design of Krasnaya Moskva, created by Andrei Yevseyev and produced by the Soviet trust TeZhe. Russia found its own way to 'create the fundamental requisites of civilization', just as Lenin had declared. And yet, the two different forms of modernity in this divided world had more in common than they knew.[30]

Departure from the *belle époque* and clothes for the New Woman: Chanel's and Lamanova's double revolution

Everything in Moscow and Paris alike pointed to a break with the past that encompassed not just the world of perfume, luxury and fashion, but society as a whole. This was a world in motion, one that had been shaken to the core by the experiences of World War I with its millions of dead and wounded, its physical and psychological traumas. In Russia, the war had been followed by revolutions and a protracted civil war that roiled the farthest reaches of the Russian Empire – or what had been the Empire. It was not just a political or national order that had collapsed, it was an entire way of life. War and revolution were a catastrophic catalyst for all the processes that had been brewing long before these events took place, the 'life reform' projects that had ripened on the vine of the *belle époque* – though Russia shot clear past the goal of reform and landed instead on a comprehensive life revolution. For all of the regional differences, ridding oneself of the old and paving the way for the new was a base note found throughout post-war Europe. It was about 'the whole', not the details. It was about a new concept of humanity, about the changing role of women and gender relations, about authority and the hierarchy of power, about a different relationship with work and leisure, about a new awareness of the body.

It is no surprise, then, that nearly identical ideas about the future contours of a better and more beautiful life emerged almost simultaneously everywhere in Europe, not just in Russia and France. It was Walter Benjamin in his study of Paris, 'capital of the nineteenth century', who accorded fashion a central role as an indicator of these processes. Fashion, according to Benjamin in his monumental – but ultimately incomplete – work, preempts and hints at the future:

> For the philosopher, the most interesting thing about fashion is its extraordinary anticipations. It is well known that art will often – for example, in pictures – precede the perceptible reality by years. It was possible to see streets or rooms that shone in all sorts of fiery colors long before technology, by means of illuminated signs and other arrangements, actually set them under such a light. Moreover, the sensitivity of the individual artist to what is coming certainly far exceeds that of the *grande dame*. Yet fashion is in much steadier, much more precise contact with the coming thing, thanks to the incomparable nose which the feminine collective has for what lies waiting in the future. Each season brings, in its newest creations, various secret signals of things to come. Whoever understands how to read these semaphores would know in advance not only about new currents in the arts but also about new legal codes, wars, and revolutions. – Here, surely, lies the greatest charm of fashion, but also the difficulty of making the charming fruitful.[1]

The 'paradigm shift' that Chanel's biographer Edmonde Charles-Roux identified in the creation of Chanel No. 5 took place in fashion as a whole. What is astonishing here is just how close the resemblance is between the formulations for the style of the future à la Chanel and the style of the New Woman as imagined by Nadezhda Lamanova, the 'real professional of Russian fashion' (Alexandre Vassiliev) in the 1920s and 1930s.[2]

Gabrielle Chanel – to refer to Coco Chanel by her actual name – was not the only trailblazer. Paul Poiret, a pioneer in the French fashion industry before World War I, had also done important groundwork. 'But now, with Chanel, ornamentation was suddenly giving way to "line"; a garment had appeared that was determined solely by the logic of a creator grappling with necessity.' It was Gabrielle Chanel, however, who reached the point of no return in 1916 and made a decisive break with all that had come before. She wrote that 'women had the right to be comfortable, to move about freely in their clothes; style became more important, to the detriment of adornment; and lastly, "poor" materials were suddenly ennobled, which automatically made possible the rapid growth of fashion within reach of the majority.' As a result, 'for the first time a revolution in feminine attire, far from following any whims or caprices, consisted essentially and unavoidably in abolishing them'. This was because 'you couldn't do a thing' with jersey fabric:

> One dart, the slightest tension, and the threads, too loosely worked, would unravel. Anyone else would have given up. Gabrielle dug in her heels. Simplify, that was the only way. The shirtwaist dress stopped well above the ankle. With one stroke Gabrielle annihilated the centuries-old gesture so many men had breathlessly awaited as a woman prepared to mount a step: the discreet lifting of the skirt. A certain form of femininity was ending – that of the thousand-pleated bodice and the cascades of veiling on the hat.

Gone was the woman who 'allowed the long train of her mauve gown to spread behind her'. In her place was a person who stepped out unimpeded and could dress and undress herself in a flash, someone to be wary of:

> Commentators were understandably discouraged by the newcomer. . . . She was an absolutely new woman, a woman whose dress was *without allusion*. Pointless to interrogate her. The rules of the game had been deliberately muddled. What attitude was one to take toward a fashion the key to which could not be found in any museum? However much erudition one might deploy, this woman was beyond belief.[3]

Harper's Bazaar covered Chanel's first collection in 1916, but it would be a full decade before the American edition of *Vogue* claimed that Chanel had finally found the form of the quintessential modern woman's dress – a parallel to the form she had found for perfume. It was a dress 'disconcerting in its simplicity', almost a uniform, collarless, made of black crêpe de Chine with 'long, very tight-fitting sleeves, and bloused above the hips, which were closely hugged by the skirt' – Chanel's 'little black dress', practical, comfortable, elegant.[4]

The belief that clothing, and women's clothing in particular, should be devoid of all ornament and designed for comfort and function had been formulated in a practically programmatic way at the same time by the leading Soviet couturier, Nadezhda Lamanova. She said that clothing should do no violence to the body – it should not force anything, but instead be in accordance with the body. 'The new costume will be in line with the new life: working, dynamic, and aware.'[5] In her 'On the Rationality of Costume', Lamanova writes:

> Costume is one of the most sensitive manifestations of social life and psychology. The unprecedented categorical restructuring of the entire social organism and the birth of the new mass consumer in Soviet Russia inevitably bring in their wake an equally sharp change

of costume. Hence the necessity of creating a new costume that combines the artistic sense of form peculiar to our epoch with the purely practical requirements of our time. In contrast to West European fashion, whose changes depend on commercial considerations, we must assume as a basis of our costume considerations of social hygiene, the requirements of work, etc. It is not enough to create merely a comfortable costume; we need to ensure a proper correlation between the artistic elements of costume and the new forms and aspirations of the emerging new life. All these conditions require methods of artistic construction and practical realization of contemporary costume in the interests of mass production. Costume is in a sense a continuation of the body. It has functions to perform, like our bodies, in life and in work, and this is why clothes must be rational – they must not hinder the wearer, but in fact help him. Hence the most important factors dictating clothes design are the following:

1) The wearer's personal mood and taste in one form or another (the wearer's style).
2) The style of the epoch; its cultural physiognomy.
3) The form of the individual expressed in a definite silhouette.
4) The fabric, which, being in itself a given form, predetermines some of the elements of the shape we are creating.
5) The utilitarian purpose of the costume.

Thus, the task of creating an artistic costume involves the integration of the figure, the fabric and the purpose into a common form as appealing as possible in the eyes of the epoch and the wearer. The above can be expressed in the practical formula:

For whom
From what
For what purpose
and all this is synthesized in *how* (the form).

In creating the form according to these principles, it is necessary to observe its strict subordination to the plastic laws of proportions and relationships which govern any art. Such an interpretation of costume not only reflects the purely external life of society but also impels one to scrutinize the domestic, psychological, historical, and national features of the Russian people; this, naturally, will lead to research into folk art, as manifested in the handicraft industry. Here will be found ample opportunity to use the splendor of folk art motifs and their profound rationality so in keeping with the Soviet way of life. Traditional embroidery, laces, and linen fabrics are combined with the contemporary sense of form brought into existence by the renewed social and psychological life of society.[6]

Her combination of utility and aesthetic sophistication was probably the secret to Lamanova's elevation to the *haute couturière* of the Soviet Union. She withstood the reckoning with the Formalists and Constructivists in the early 1930s, whose original and fantastic creations she had played no part in, and then established the House of Prototypes in 1935, laying the institutional foundation for the development of Soviet fashion in the planned economy.[7]

Both the aesthetic kinship and the difference between the two fashion designers can probably be attributed in part to the women's comparable but different life trajectories. But, above all, they can be traced back to a particular 'temporal home', the period in which Europe bade farewell to the *belle époque* after the Great War and set out for a new and unfamiliar 'modernity'.

Gabrielle Chanel, born in 1883 in Saumur in the Maine-et-Loire *département*, was the illegitimate daughter of a street vendor who travelled from market to market. She spent her adolescence in an orphanage run by nuns from the convent of Aubazine, and later

5 Nadezhda Lamanova, 1880s

attended a Catholic girls' school in Moulins.[8] Chanel
learned to sew early on. Nadezhda Lamanova belonged
to an earlier generation. She was born in 1861 to an
impoverished noble family near Moscow. She attended

6 Fashion design by Nadezhda Lamanova

the girls' school in Nizhny Novgorod and then trained
in a dressmaking school in Moscow. By the start of
the twentieth century, Lamanova was already a highly
sought-after seamstress and soon to become a purveyor
to Her Imperial Highness.

Both women experienced dramatic phases of life that brought them into contact with a wide variety of worlds. Chanel was a seamstress as well as a singer in a café in Moulins. Singing brought her into the orbit of the resort town of Vichy, and she began to move in milieus far removed from her provincial origins, thanks to her connections with lovers from 'higher' social circles: the cavalry officer and textile heir Étienne Balsan, with whom she lived in a chateau, and his friend Arthur Edward 'Boy' Capel, an upper-class Englishman who helped her to establish fashion boutiques in the chic seaside resorts of Deauville and Biarritz, and eventually in Paris. Lamanova had led a cosmopolitan existence even before World War I and visited Paris regularly. Chanel became cosmopolitan in part through her generous lovers (though she never relinquished her independence), but mainly through her achievements – indeed, through her genius.

Both women were involved in the arts, particularly theatre. Lamanova worked as a costume designer at Konstantin Stanislavsky's Moscow Art Theatre, while Chanel's association with Misia Sert, queen of the bohemian scene in Paris, brought her into contact with Parisian society and the most important personalities in the Ballets Russes – Sergei Diaghilev above all. After the Russian Revolution, Lamanova was temporarily imprisoned with her husband in 1919, but she was released again when Maxim Gorky intervened on her behalf. She was subsequently a key figure in the Soviet fashion industry until her death in 1941. Chanel worked in a hospital for a while during World War I and became a key figure in the French fashion scene after the war.[9] Both had directly experienced the gulf and tension between 'ordinary people' with their 'common-sense understanding of art' and refined high culture as represented by the Ballets Russes and the Moscow Art Theatre, and they both put that experience to productive use.

Chanel, according to her biographer, always remembered her parents' 'penchant for everything clean, fresh, of good quality'. The orphanage in Aubazine where she grew up would manifest itself in her most spectacular creation, the little black dress.

> White the orphans' blouses, washed and washed again, always clean. Black their skirts, box-pleated to last, and to allow them to take long strides. Black the nuns' veils and wide-sleeve robes . . . with a cuff deep enough to hide a handkerchief. But white the starched band around their heads and the wide wimple in the form of a ruff. White, too, the long corridors, and the whitewashed walls, but black the tall dormitory doors, a black so deep, so noble that if ever you see it, that black stays in your memory forever.

School left its traces on her as well: 'Two details, insignificant at first sight, were to stick in her memory forever: the collars of the rue du Lycée schoolboys with their floppy bow ties, and the black of their smocks.' In Vichy, where she worked as a milliner, she already gave the impression of being someone who had been 'saved, by a miracle, from the absurdities of the day' and who impressed others with her 'divine simplicity of effect'.[10]

From every space she traversed, Chanel absorbed something that would ultimately characterize her style: practicality and simplicity from her childhood; sportiness from the horse races, tennis courts, seaside resorts and excursions on rich men's yachts; the striped shirts of sailors; the jackets of fishermen; the embroidered tunics of Russian peasants. She made a virtue of necessity and pivoted to using jersey fabrics during the war, creating a new style in the process. But no price was too high when it came to perfection, as was the case when she chose the formula for Chanel No. 5. She took inspiration from the set and costume designers of the Ballets Russes, but her own fashions appeared on the stage as well. The ballet *Le train bleu* by Jean Cocteau, Darius Milhaud and Sergei Diaghilev, which premiered on 20 June 1924 and revolved around a love affair at the beach, featured beachgoers, tennis players and golf champions attired not in theatrical costumes but actual bathing costumes and clothes designed by Chanel – a cast of athletes with bare legs, in tennis and golf shoes.[11] Chanel's motto was 'Always take away, always pare down. Never add . . . There is no beauty without freedom of the body.'[12] As sophisticated a man as Harry Graf Kessler noted on 24 June 1924, after the premiere, that the ballet was a display of 'magical transformations of the most modern life, the metamorphosis of everyday life, and above all modern sport, into poetry: tennis players, acrobats, gymnasts, wrestlers, swimmers.' He wrote enthusiastically of the 'frieze-like groupings', the 'images of great, enthralling beauty' which 'seemed at once Greek and hyper-modern'.[13]

Nadezhda Lamanova inhabited an environment in which clothing and fashion had explicitly become a question of class struggle. After the end of the Russian Civil War, the routines of everyday life returned and the clothing and textile industry got back on its feet – and fashion along with it; the Kersten knitwear factory became the Red Banner factory.[14] The 1920s were a fight over clothing for the New Woman, the outcome of which was in no way predetermined. It was the chaotic situation of the New Economic Policy that gifted the world one of the most fascinating chapters in the history of twentieth-century style. The disarray of a decade of war, revolution and civil war gave way to an explosion of creativity in which the remnants of pre-revolutionary fashion were resurrected and the battle over fashionable forms was deliberately fought as a battle between the classes, between old and new, past and future. As the old establishments, cinemas and cabarets filled up again overnight – with 'former people' and the new 'NEP

7 Scene from *Le train bleu* by Jean Cocteau

bourgeoisie' – the trappings of pre-war fashion returned
as well and were updated for the ever-popular dances:
the tango, the foxtrot, the two-step. The scenes were not
all that different from those painted by George Grosz
in Berlin in the 'Roaring Twenties', with sequinned
dresses, plunging necklines, feather boas, evening gowns
with sleek silhouettes and no waistline, long cigarette holders, stoles, clothing that tended to emphasize

androgynous and metrosexual elements, unlike the muscular proletarian shapes of war communism.

Early on, in 1919, after the first Soviet sewing laboratory had been founded, Nadezhda Lamanova outlined her vision for a departure from these fashions of the lost world. Revolutionary clothing was not to be sumptuous and luxurious but, instead, practical above all. It was to be free of all extraneous decoration – embellishments, ornaments, overly expensive material – and should contribute to the elevation of everyday culture, not for a specific wealthy class of people, but for the entire population. Women were to step out of their role as accoutrements or ornaments for men. The main experimental field for this clothing for the New Woman was the theatre, where prototypes could be presented on stage. There is a path here leading from the costume designers of the Ballets Russes to the extravagant set designs and costumes of the Soviet avant-garde, as featured in productions by Nikolai Evreinov, Vsevolod Meyerhold and Alexander Tairov. Even the abstract-geometric costumes in the science-fiction film *Aelita* (1924), based on a novel by Alexei Tolstoy, could be viewed as a demonstration of avant-garde fashion. Painters who had been intent on the radical reduction of forms, such as Varvara Stepanova and Lyubov Popova, now distinguished themselves as textile and clothing designers, and, in doing so, they looked to the colours and contours found in Russian folk art and folklore.[15]

These two parallel, and yet very different, lines of production converged at the Exposition Internationale des Arts Décoratifs et Industriels Modernes in Paris in 1925. A quarter of a century after the great world expo of 1900, this exhibition was meant to demonstrate the leading role and rebirth of France after the end of the devastating war. The programme was extremely ambitious; only the very latest art and technology were to be exhibited. For obvious political reasons, representatives of the German Reich were not invited, but an invitation was extended to the Soviet Union, whose pavilion attracted the most attention. Millions of visitors to the Grand Palais and the pavilions between the Place de la Concorde and Place Alma were treated to a rich display of contemporary art. The focus was on architecture and design, and the pavilions developed by Konstantin Melnikov and Le Corbusier were tremendously popular. But the graphic design, poster art and fashion associated with names such as El Lissitzky, Alexander Rodchenko and Nadezhda Lamanova were big draws as well. Textiles, garments, toys and jewellery made from the simplest materials enthralled the Western public and were rewarded with grand prizes and numerous medals – all in an atmosphere that was generally open towards Soviet Russia, from which great things had been expected.[16]

The expo of 1925 left Art Nouveau behind. Bauhaus was all the rage now (even though no one from Germany was officially invited), and everyone was talking about Le Corbusier, Cubism, art inspired by the excavations in Egypt and Mexico. The expo gave its name to the new epoch: Art Deco. Paul Poiret, who had founded his own fashion and perfume company in 1922, played a perfume piano on a barge named *Amours*, which wafted fragrances through the air. There was also a 'Palais des Elégances', which was remarkable because it brought together:

> the gowns of Jean Patou, Chanel, Jeanne Lanvin, and Louise Boulanger, and displayed them along with Poiret's fabrics, with silks and lighting appliances, Lalique crystal, Dunand's laquerwork, Christofle's gold and silver, ironwork and porcelains, French and foreign; the only unifying condition was that the lines of gowns and forms of objects must be clean, their ornamentation sober, and their relief unexaggerated. The Arts Déco was an undisputed success.[17]

It was the colourful folkloric elements and contemporary fascination with all things exotic, foreign and 'primitive', on the one hand, and the radicalness of the production aesthetic, on the other, that drew so much attention to Soviet design, fashion and architecture at the expo.

And what did the expo of 1925 mean for Chanel? The designs and accessories she presented caused a sensation worldwide. In 1926, American *Vogue* called Chanel's little black dress 'the Chanel Ford' in reference to the American automobile manufacturer. With his functionally attractive car, Ford had turned a luxury object into an affordable product for many people – and with her simple and elegant little black dress, Chanel had created a 'Ford signed Chanel'.[18] Lamanova, too, stood for a type of fashion that combined taste and quality and was intended to be accessible even to ordinary people, thanks to mass production. Ford was a reference point for French *haute couture*, on the one hand, and Ford was the embodiment of the Soviet industrialization project, on the other – there were Ford tractors on collective farms, and the motor city of Nizhny Novgorod was dubbed the 'Russian Detroit'. These signs indicated that a third major player was already on the horizon: America.

Chanel's Russian connection

It was not a forgone conclusion that a milliner and modiste, however talented, would make the acquaintance of social figures – particularly men – who would clear the way for her to leave her little world and enter the great big one. A space had to exist in which a hatmaker like Chanel could not only meet someone like Boy Capel, the rich lover who helped her to open her first boutiques, but could also strike up relationships with Georges Clemenceau, prime minister of France, and Winston Churchill, whose finest hour was still to come. Places had to exist where a fashion designer could encounter the Duke of Westminster, the richest man in Britain, whose country estates Chanel would often stay at, and where she could also meet a member of the tsar's family who recalled knowing a perfumer back in Saint Petersburg before the revolution.

There was a place where the world of the *belle époque* gathered with all of its rituals, habits and money. There was a place where the castaways of a society lost to war and revolution had taken refuge. There was a place that the most sensitive characters of the age – artists, literati and painters from all over the world – flocked to when they wanted to be on the cutting edge and at the centre of the action. This place was Paris, 'capital of the nineteenth century', which emerged from the catastrophe of World War I to shine in all of its glory once more, before the centre of action moved to the New World. Of all the world's fairs that had been held since the mid nineteenth century, the exhibitions of 1900, 1925 and 1937 in Paris certainly left the greatest impression on the public. There was the Eiffel Tower, a demonstration of unprecedented technological advancement in the midst of the *fin-de-siècle* fair; the expo of 1925, with its ambition to embrace the changed world that had arisen from the 'great seminal catastrophe' of the twentieth century; and the exhibition of 1937, where the pavilions of the Soviet Union and Germany stepped from the shadow of the Eiffel Tower and pointed to a new dimension of monumentality and totality.

Millions flocked to the city to catch a glimpse of the world and its future. Rentiers arrived, and the idle rich of the 'world of yesterday' (Stefan Zweig),[1] the connoisseurs of luxury and fashion who could afford anything – all those who had an inkling that something monstrous was brewing beneath the varnish of the well-ordered world. There were utopians, apocalypticists, hysterics, prophets, experimenters, people in touch with sub-surface sentiments and currents, who picked up the signals reaching Europe from all over the world of liberation movements, revolts, massacres, assassinations, natural disasters and undreamt-of inventions. Tourists came from around the globe, wanting to see once again what Europe had achieved in its best times.[2] Africans arrived, and Asians, who listened carefully to what was said in the universities, academies and cafés and, in doing so, learned to free themselves of Europe. There were Americans such as Ernest Hemingway and Gertrude Stein, who wandered the Louvre in search of themselves and the 'Lost Generation', and who took up residence in the cafés only to find that the Americans still had their own way of life ahead of them. There were English and Germans, too, who naturally spoke perfect French and wanted to take something of this finer European lifestyle back home with them.[3]

But it was the Russians, above all, who made their first major appearance as a European cultural superpower in Paris. In Paris, on foreign soil, beyond the borders of Russia, people who might never have otherwise met encountered one another after the revolution. All of them together made up the Russian scene that would exert an extraordinary influence on its environment, before and after the war, before and after the great revolution.

Paris stood alongside Italy as the most important destination for Russian travellers prior to World War I. Aristocrats had been drawn to the seaside resorts on the Mediterranean with some regularity. Year after year, Russian colonies sprang up on the Côte d'Azur in Cannes, San Remo, Antibes and Nice, and on the Atlantic in Biarritz and Deauville, catered to by a service and luxury industry of the highest standards, one which included Russian Orthodox churches and synagogues. The resorts suffered a heavy economic blow when these wealthy tourists disappeared after the war began, and especially after the Russian Revolution. Educational tourism was a rapidly growing sector, and Paris was the highlight of a traveller's Grand Tour through Europe. The topography of tourist attractions, hotels and other establishments has been preserved in the Russian guidebooks of the age. The expansion of the railway network, especially the Nord Express from Saint Petersburg to Paris, intensified communication and exchange between two worlds that had previously been very far apart.[4]

Ever since the French Revolution, France had additionally been a refuge for political dissidents and freedom fighters from all over the world, and nineteenth-century Paris became a place of exile for Russian revolutionaries and place of study for members of the intelligentsia. Revolutionary democrats and oppositionists of all stripes turned Paris (along with London and Geneva) into a locus of anti-tsarist resistance, a publishing centre, a meeting place and a training ground.

Every new trend in art seemed to appear in Paris before any other European metropolis, from Impressionism, Secessionism and Symbolism to the various strains of Dadaism and Surrealism later on. Everyone went to Paris – from Saint Petersburg, Riga, Kiev and Warsaw – which is why epoch-making artists and Russian intellectuals could be found here years before the Russian Revolution: Marc Chagall from Vitebsk, Alexandra Exter from Kiev, Mikhail Larionov from Moscow. At the end of the twentieth century, the works of these representatives of the 'School of Paris' would be rediscovered and displayed in major exhibitions such as 'Paris–Moscou 1900–1930' at the Centre Pompidou.[5]

One highlight of this Russian presence in Paris and its global influence was the 'Saisons Russes' of the Ballets Russes, founded by all-round genius and impresario Sergei Diaghilev. Diaghilev – who, before leaving Russia in 1906, had been director of the Imperial Theatre in Saint Petersburg, a curator of exhibitions and initiator of a leading art journal – achieved nothing less than the creation of a magnificent *Gesamtkunstwerk* involving artists from every discipline: music, dance, writing, painting. He worked with the composers Igor Stravinsky, Darius Milhaud, Erik Satie and Sergei Prokofiev; the choreographers and dancers Léonide Massine, Serge Lifar, Boris Kochno and Vaslav Nijinsky; the ballerinas Anna Pavlova, Tamara Karsavina and Bronislava Nijinska; the painters Pablo Picasso, Juan Gris, Fernand Léger, Salvador Dalí, Léon Bakst and Alexandre Benois – and the costume designer Gabrielle Chanel.

The 'Saisons Russes' featured premieres that made music history: *The Rite of Spring*, *The Firebird*, *The Love for Three Oranges*, *Les Noces* (*The Wedding*), *Le Pas d'Acier*. The performances were not just artistic,

8 Sergei Diaghilev painted by Léon Bakst, 1906

they were social events to which audiences flocked
from around the world. Sergei Diaghilev toured almost
constantly with his company, visiting Paris, Monte
Carlo, London, Berlin, Vienna, Budapest, Buenos Aires,
New York. It was Gabrielle Coco Chanel who made it

possible for Diaghilev to revive the production of *The Rite of Spring* in 1920 with a donation of 300,000 francs, and it was Chanel who travelled to Venice in 1929 to see the dying Diaghilev and arrange a worthy wake and burial for him. Chanel invited Stravinsky and his family to stay at Bel Respiro, her villa in Garches, when the composer was moving from Switzerland to France. And she offered refuge in Biarritz to Grand Duke Dmitri Pavlovich, a member of the Romanov dynasty living an impoverished existence in France. High-society women who had fled Russia after the revolution now worked for Chanel as models, modistes and experts in precious materials and accessories.[6] Chanel was surrounded by 'Russian things' and felt deeply connected to the elegant 'former people' with their sureness of taste and cultivation.

Salons were where the Russian and international world met and mingled with Parisian society, and the leading salon in this respect was hosted by the legendary Misia Sert, daughter of the Polish artist Cyprian Godebski. She had been born in Saint Petersburg, educated in the best schools and, with Gabriel Fauré as her piano teacher, seemed destined for a career as a concert pianist. Instead, Misia Sert decided to marry Thadée Natanson, editor of an influential journal, whom she eventually left to marry a wealthy English lover, one Mr Edwards, whom she divorced ten years later for the Catalan-born Josep Maria Sert, a painter who became very successful in Paris and the United States; he painted the frescoes in New York's Waldorf-Astoria hotel, in the Palace of Nations in Geneva and in the Vatican pavilion at the Paris expo of 1937. *Tout-Paris* frequented the salon run by Misia Natanson / Mrs Edwards: Henri de Toulouse-Lautrec, Maurice Ravel, Erik Satie, Paul Verlaine, Marcel Proust, Jean Cocteau. Portraits of her were painted by Pierre Bonnard and Félix Vallotton. Misia was deeply impressed by Chanel, a kindred spirit, and it was she who introduced Chanel to Diaghilev. Misia remained close to Chanel to the end of her life.[7]

France was Russia's ally in World War I and became the country of choice for emigrants fleeing the Russian Empire after the defeat of the anti-Bolshevik forces. Along with Constantinople, Prague, Berlin and Harbin, Paris became a centre of 'Russia abroad', with thousands of refugees living in a country just starting to recover from the severe losses of the war. It was the scene of assassinations and abductions; members of the White Army were kidnapped by Soviet intelligence services and taken back to the Soviet Union, and representatives of the anti-Stalinist left-wing opposition, including Trotsky's son Lev Sedov, were hunted by Soviet agents. Paris was the site of countless individual tragedies amongst people who had lost everything and were forced to start over. Army officers worked as taxi drivers or labourers in the Renault factories in Boulogne-Billancourt, aristocrats and governesses were employed as seamstresses and saleswomen. The Russian emigrants had their own infrastructure, with schools, newspapers and publishing houses, religious congregations and youth camps. 'New Mecca, New Babylon' is how historian Robert H. Johnston referred to Russian Paris.[8]

Social scenes and family relations formed at this hub, marriages took place: Picasso's marriage to Olga Khokhlova, Romain Rolland's marriage to Maria Kudasheva, Fernand Léger's marriage to Nadia Khodasevich, and the relationships entertained by Gala (actually Elena Diakonova), spouse and muse to Paul Éluard and Salvador Dalí, mistress and muse to Max Ernst – none of these were exotic exceptions. Transnational tastes and styles amalgamated here.

Ernest Beaux is a fairly typical example of someone who crossed borders as a matter of course throughout his life. He was born in Moscow, socialized in Russia, trained at the French perfume company Rallet, and returned to his 'first home' after the revolution. Gabrielle Chanel and Ernest Beaux were brought together by Grand Duke Dmitri Pavlovich Romanov, a long-time resident of France, grandson to Alexander II, nephew to Alexander III, cousin to the last tsar, raised with his sister in the Kremlin by English nurses and by an uncle who served as Governor-General of Moscow before being assassinated by a terrorist. Harry Graf Kessler – an outside observer, but one who was intimately acquainted with the Paris scene – described the liaison between Chanel and Dmitri Pavlovich by saying that Dmitri had 'thrown away the imperial crown through his life in Paris'. Kessler wrote that Dmitri had immediately taken up with 'a filthy rich cocotte and seamstress named Chanelle, known as "Coco", a friend of my old friend Missia Edwards (Sert) and has come into money again through this liaison; i.e., he is being kept by "Coco"'. Kessler additionally wrote of 'Diaghilev, who has also become intimate with Coco and lets her "lend" him money for his ballet', and of the grand parties held by 'Coco', where she and Misia set the tone: 'receptions with caviar, foie gras, fruits, big hams' (diary entry from 16 January 1924).[9] Rarely was the otherwise so precise and perceptive Count Kessler so wrong in his assessment of his European acquaintances as he was in the case of Chanel.

The close connection between Coco Chanel and the Russian scene is also apparent in her direct co-operation with the founder of the Kitmir fashion *atelier*, Grand Duchess Maria Pavlovna. Charles-Roux writes:

A body-hugging *rubashka* done in thin wool and worn over a straight skirt, with discreetly embroidered bands on collar and cuffs – a garment, in short, whose feel came entirely from the Russian soil but whose form was pure Parisian. . . . The *rubashka* idea worked so well that

she [Chanel] set up an embroidery workshop. Grand
Duchess Maria was put in charge of it.[10]

Kitmir, named after a mythical Persian creature, was
also present at the 1925 expo and was one of the many
fashion *ateliers* founded by Russian emigrants in the
1920s in Paris and other centres of emigration, including Berlin and Harbin in the Far East. Maria Pavlovna
Romanova, unhappily married to a Swedish prince
before World War I, had fled Russia after the revolution via Kiev, Odessa, Constantinople, Bucharest and
London, finally settling in Paris, where in 1921, through
her brother Dmitri Pavlovich, she met Coco Chanel.
Though traumatized by the fate of her nearest kin –
her father had been executed in Saint Petersburg, and
other close relatives were murdered in Crimea – she had
established her own fashion *atelier* with a great deal of
determination and entrepreneurial skill.

Other big names from the Russian aristocracy – the
Obolenskys, Yusupovs, Dolgorukys, Bakhmetyevs –
could also be found in the Parisian fashion scene of
the time. These society figures from Saint Petersburg
and Moscow were well acquainted with the world
of luxury and fashion. And, thanks to their governesses, their first language was often not Russian, but
French. Russian beauties were the epitome of elegance.
Models such as Gali Bazhenova, Nyusha Rotwand and
Lady Abdi graced the pages of *Harper's Bazaar* and
Vogue, their pictures snapped by leading fashion photo-
graphers including Alexander Liberman and Baron
George Hoyningen-Huene, or drawn by famous fashion
illustrators like Erté (actually Roman Tyrtov: 'R. T.').
With creations as expensive as they were exotic –
embroideries, tiaras in the shape of Russian *kokoshniks*,
shapkas, shawls and coats made of costly furs, beaded
necklaces and belts, dolls dressed in folk costumes, par-
asols, extravagant little bags – Russian designs aligned

9 Kitmir Broderie poster

with Western projections of the enigmatic East and ful-
filled a widespread desire for exclusive beauty.[11]

Women such as Maria Pavlovna were often able to
deal better with the hardships of exile than the men who
had lost their positions and status. The tough lessons of
exile had turned many into true survivors who proved
themselves in new fields – Maria Pavlovna, for instance,

also created her own perfume by the name of Prince Igor – and who set out to conquer the American market as well. There is a good deal of evidence that Chanel's distaste for Bolshevism was driven more by aesthetics than politics. All that Paris, 'capital of the nineteenth century', had once exported to Saint Petersburg and Moscow now found its way back to the city along the routes taken by Russian refugees and émigrés. The refugees included prominent Russian entrepreneurs and art patrons who had bought paintings by Picasso, Matisse, van Gogh and Cézanne and displayed them in their homes long before these artists achieved worldwide success. And while the legendary Russian art collectors Sergei Shchukin and Ivan Morozov left Russia and died abroad (Shchukin in Paris in 1935, Morozov in Karlovy Vary in 1921), their collections of modern French art – the largest in the world at the time – were appropriated by the Bolshevik government and nationalized. They remain in Russia to this day, popular attractions at the Hermitage and the Pushkin Museum and reminders of the Paris–Moscow axis in the grand age of European modernity.[12]

French connection in Moscow? The 'fatherland of workers' and traces of Mikhail Bulgakov

While Russian aristocrats, bourgeois intellectuals and members of the White Army had fled the revolution and taken refuge in Paris, those who hoped the Russian Revolution would bring about a new world were drawn eastwards instead, to Moscow. Revolutionary Russia initially represented, above all, an escape from the 'storm of steel' of the Great War. The fall of the tsarist government and then the Provisional Government offered the prospect of an end to the carnage that had killed millions of people in Europe and maimed thousands upon thousands, leaving an entire generation eager to find some way back to a peaceful life. The hope that the revolution would end war once and for all attracted sympathizers and Party supporters to revolutionary Russia from all over Europe, including authors writing in a 'Christian communist' vein, such as Pierre Pascal, and proponents of a radical pacifism, such as Henri Barbusse. Barbusse in particular, a wounded war veteran and author of *Le feu*, remained devoted to the country until his death in 1935. He was working on a biography of Stalin right until the end.[1]

78

The 'heat flow' of pacifism had also carried Romain Rolland, an author famous even before the war, to Russia later in his life, where he paid a courtesy visit to Stalin. An idealism that allowed one to overlook many of the absurdities of Soviet reality – and that would later veer into a bizarre apologia for the Stalinist dictatorship – was the driving force behind the Moscow tourism of many bourgeois humanists and pacifists, including André Gide. But even someone like Louis-Ferdinand Céline did not want to miss out.

The militant socialists who had split off from the Second International and formed a party in the Communist International were of another type altogether. For them, Moscow was not the party of peace but the party of civil war. They viewed Soviet Russia as the start of a great experiment, and they had no reservations about accepting the leadership of the Bolshevik Party, even on an international scale. Co-founders of the French Communist Party, such as Paul Vaillant-Couturier and Maurice Thorez, who came and went from Moscow, were well known – and, indeed, popular – Party leaders in France in their time. Paul Vaillant-Couturier published an account of his travels through Soviet Russia, *Les bâtisseurs de la vie nouvelle: neuf mois de voyage dans l'URSS du plan quinquennal*, in 1932.[2]

But perhaps the most influential figures along the Paris–Moscow axis were the fellow travellers who had nothing to do with communism in the strictest sense (meaning in terms of Party programmes or membership obligations), but who were vaguely sympathetic towards the Soviet experiment, fascinated by the attempt to try out a new form of social life, and, above all, viewed the Soviet Union as an ally against capitalism and the impending war. They generally had no real understanding of the Soviet Union, which was more of a dreamland and projection *ex negativo* of the capitalist environment they knew and opposed. Soviet Russia might not have been perfect, so their thinking went, but at least it was trying to do something – and, in any case, it was the lesser evil.

Many wanted to see for themselves what was happening there, with even the young Christian Dior and already-famous Elsa Schiaparelli setting out for the East. Others took the opportunity to actually participate, including Le Corbusier, who entered the design competition for the Palace of Soviets and even completed a project in Moscow (together with his Soviet colleague Nikolai Kolli): the construction of the building that now houses the Central Statistics Office.[3] Regular commuters between Paris and Moscow included Louis Aragon and his wife, Elsa Triolet, whose sister, Lilya Brik, was the lover of Vladimir Mayakovsky and host of one of the most important salons in the Stalin era. André Malraux, Jean-Richard Bloch and Paul Nizan attended the First Congress of Soviet Writers in 1934; Louis-Ferdinand Céline visited Leningrad in 1937 and reported on his trip in an antisemitic pamphlet entitled *Bagatelles pour un massacre*. One writer who took his own trip to the Soviet Union very seriously was André Gide, who had stood at the balustrade of the mausoleum in 1936 to take in the parade of young athletes but subsequently revised his naïve image of the country, bringing down upon himself the hatred of left-wingers loyal to Moscow.[4] A high point of these French–Russian encounters was the First International Congress of Writers for the Defence of Culture in Paris in 1935, which attracted Anna Seghers, Heinrich and Klaus Mann, Bertolt Brecht and Lion Feuchtwanger, as well as noted writers such as Ilya Ehrenburg and Boris Pasternak from the Soviet Union. But events in Moscow – first the show trials with their ridiculous self-incriminations and the execution of prominent revolutionaries, then the moral collapse triggered in 1939 by the Molotov–Ribbentrop Pact

– finally brought an end to the old left of the popular front.[5]

Traces of the relationship that had been forged between Paris and Moscow over many decades can be found, paradoxically, in Mikhail Bulgakov's novel *The Master and Margarita*, which Bulgakov began writing in the NEP years and finished in the 1930s. The relevant chapter in the novel is 'Black Magic and its Exposé'.[6] It opens with a variety show featuring a clown, a blonde dancer in a short skirt and tights, and the pale, powdered master of ceremonies, George Bengalsky, who introduces the performance of Monsieur Woland, a magician accompanied by a tall fellow named Fagot and a fat black cat. From the stage, they explain that they want to find out how the people of Moscow have changed, outwardly and inwardly. All manner of tricks follow: roubles flutter from the ceiling, and the cat tears off Bengalsky's head but then plops it back in place. For the next trick, the stage is transformed into an *atelier* clearly modelled on a fashion boutique in Paris. At the end of the performance, the scene is overrun by women grabbing dresses. Bulgakov brings a piece of Paris to the stage:

> Suddenly the stage floor was covered with Persian rugs, huge mirrors appeared, illuminated along the sides by elongated green bulbs, and between the mirrors were glass display cases where the audience, in a state of happy bedazzlement, beheld Parisian frocks in various colors and styles. These were in some of the cases, and in others were hundreds of hats, with feathers and without, and hundreds of shoes, with buckles and without – black, white, yellow, leather, satin, suede, shoes with straps and shoes with gems. Containers of perfume appeared among the shoes, as well as mountains of chamois, satin, and silk handbags with piles of elongated, embossed gold lipstick cases scattered between them.

The devil only knows where the red-haired girl in the black evening dress came from, who was standing by the display cases with a proprietary smile, her beauty marred only by a strange scar on her neck.

With a saccharine smile, Fagot announced to the women in the audience that the store would exchange their old clothes and shoes for Parisian styles and Parisian shoes. He added that the same sort of exchange would apply to handbags and the like.

The cat scraped his hind paw and, simultaneously, gestured with his front paw, the way doormen do upon opening the door.

Sweetly, albeit with a touch of throatiness, the redhead began to recite words which were baffling but seductive, judging by the women's faces in the orchestra, '*Guerlain*, *Chanel No. 5*, *Mitsouko*, *Narcisse Noir*, evening gowns, cocktail dresses . . .'

Fagot twisted and squirmed, the cat bowed, and the girl opened the glass cases.

'Be our guests!' bellowed Fagot. 'No need to be shy or stand on ceremony!'

Women in the audience stand up and come to the stage. As a souvenir of the evening, they are given a bottle of perfume to take home. '"The firm asks you to accept this as a memento," said Fagot, handing her an open box with a bottle of perfume inside. // "*Merci*," the brunette answered haughtily, and she went back down to her seat. As she walked up the aisle, people jumped up, trying to touch the box.'[7]

Bulgakov obviously assumed that his readers would be familiar with Chanel No. 5. He evokes the world of the Parisian boutique, and this scent plays a major role. The audience goes into raptures, and the perfume bottle is a symbol of enchantment. The entire theatre falls into a kind of trance.

The general atmosphere of the spectacle, the behaviour

of the audience and, above all, the brand-name perfumes that are invoked recall the 1920s and the bazaar capitalism of the NEP. But the actual event in this chapter can also be read as an allegory, a play on the general confusion of the 1930s, a combination of mania, desperation and longing for salvation, a social state of trance in the tumult of the purges, in which truth and falsehood, reality and fiction could no longer be distinguished.[8]

Auguste Michel's incomplete project: a Palace of Soviets perfume

From May to November 1937, Paris once again hosted the Exposition Internationale and millions of people visited. The main attractions included the German and Soviet pavilions erected on the Champ de Mars beneath the silhouette of the Eiffel Tower. They symbolically stood for the collision of two worlds, two systems. The Soviet pavilion, designed by architect Boris Iofan, demonstratively faced off against Albert Speer's pavilion for Nazi Germany. Topped with a sculpture designed by Vera Mukhina of a worker and a *kolkhoz* woman charging forward together, the Soviet pavilion thrust skywards in opposition to the German pavilion, which had a monumental sculpture of two naked men entitled *Comradeship*, by Josef Thorak, at its entrance. Two architectures, two systems, two world views. A demonstration of the forces that would determine Europe's fate in the years to come.[1]

The year 1937 fell in the midst of a world in tumult, as the post-war order disintegrated and the contours of a pre-war period began to emerge: Mussolini's war in Abyssinia in 1935, the occupation of the Rhineland and remilitarization of Germany in 1936, the Nazis' premiere of *Olympia* in Berlin, the Austrian *Anschluss* in 1938, the anti-Jewish pogroms of 'Kristallnacht', the Munich Agreement with all of its repercussions – the annexation of the Sudetenland and demise of Czechoslovakia. In the Soviet Union, the violent collectivization of agriculture led to millions of dead, while forced industrialization and the chaos of the purges claimed hundreds of thousands of victims before Stalin secured his dictatorship once and for all. Spain was embroiled in civil war in 1937, a foretaste of the battles to come; Picasso's *Guernica* was displayed in the pavilion of the Spanish Republic at the Paris exposition. France itself was feeling the effects of the crisis following the Great Depression, and after years of mass strikes and demonstrations by right-wing extremists, the *front populaire* was in power.

In the same year – probably to coincide with the Soviet exhibition at the World's Fair – an article about the life of the perfumer Auguste Michel and the situation of the

10 Paris World Expo 1937, Soviet pavilion on
the right

Soviet perfume industry was published by the writer
Mikhail Loskutov in *Our Achievements*, a magazine
founded by Maxim Gorky. Auguste Ippolitovich Michel
(to refer to him with his patronymic) had remained in the
Soviet Union, and the article was based on an extensive
interview with him there.[2] It is a discussion of perfume
and the feelings of a lonely Frenchman in Moscow in the
time of the Great Terror and the show trials, the liquida-
tion of the 'Bolshevik guard' and the military leadership,
and, above all, the arrest and murder of hundreds of
thousands of innocents in an atmosphere rife with
rumour, suspicion and conspiracy theories concerning spies, saboteurs and fifth columns. And there sat a
native Frenchman, a 'bourgeois specialist' (*spets*) who
had long played a leading role in the Soviet perfume
industry – seemingly in the perfect position to be sucked
into the meat grinder of Stalin's purges.

Mikhail Loskutov sought out Auguste Michel at
his workplace in the New Dawn (Novaya Zarya) factory in the Zamoskvorechye district of Moscow, and
wrote a detailed portrait of the man. The laboratory in
which fragrances were composed and tested forms the
backdrop to the interview. Essences were shipped here
from all over the world to be mixed. The workrooms
were filled with bottles, chemical scales, boilers, flasks,
card files labelled with the Latin names of aromatic
substances. Employees in white smocks bustled about.
Auguste Michel sported a beard that brought to mind
the French prime minister, Georges Clemenceau. The
staff referred to Michel almost affectionately as 'our
president', 'our Michel', 'the president of perfume'.
Michel had spent his entire life in the world of scent.
He would take the paper strips for perfume samples
home with him from the office. He worked mainly with
his nose. Human emotions based on the sense of smell
are just as complex and delicate as those based on other
senses. The sense of smell is usually underestimated,

even though it is stronger and more subtle than the most sensitive chemical analysis.

Michel's sense of smell was highly trained. In his interview, Loskutov takes a detour into Michel's childhood and youth, into the period before the revolution when he worked as a perfumer for Brocard & Co. For the young generation to which Loskutov (born in 1902) belonged, the name Brocard was practically prehistorical. His contemporaries remembered the name the way they recalled the pre-revolutionary advertisements for Osman cigarettes, packages of Landrin sweets, the poster that declared 'I drink Van Houten', biscuits from the companies Einem and Georges Borman, and the compacts for the Swan Down powder produced by the house of Brocard & Co. This list could include products with names like Magnolia, Camellia and Grandmother's Bouquet, which had been created by Master Michel in a factory that now belonged to the Soviet state.

Loskutov looks back on Michel's childhood, to Cannes and the world of fragrance, sport and youth on the Côte d'Azur, to the experiences that turned the son of a locksmith into a perfumer. Michel was able to avoid military service and trained as a pharmacist, which was typical for a perfumer. He learned the craft of perfume composition from the ground up in Cannes, and then at Lamotte in Marseille. He moved to Russia, where a huge market had opened up for foreign cosmetic, pharmaceutical and perfume companies. The article recounts the story of Henri Afanasyevich Brocard, who took the risk of starting anew in Russia, a pioneer who succeeded in making a luxury product for the masses. In his conversation with Loskutov, Michel mentions the company's international awards and Henri Brocard's role as a sponsor and patron of the arts, one who had made his art collection accessible to the general public. But Michel distances himself from the all-too-perfect world depicted in Brocard's anniversary publication of

1914, which makes no mention of the labour strikes or the revolution of 1905. Instead, there are group photos of the entire staff, the hierarchy of managers, engineers, bookkeepers and workers who simulated an ideal world untouched by the reality of class warfare, and who radiated a typically bourgeois sense of self-satisfaction.

Loskutov then describes Auguste Michel's transformation from a 'citizen of the French republic' to a loyal citizen of the Soviet Union. This is also the story of Brocard's transformation into the largest socialist perfume enterprise and the transition from capitalist private industry to the socialist planned economy.

Everything starts with a mishap, which is not terribly unusual in the confusion of the revolution and civil war. The French community has already left Moscow, but Michel, who speaks fairly poor Russian, remains behind in the city. His factory is nationalized, production largely comes to a standstill, and the building is used to print Soviet bank notes instead. And then there is a stroke of bad luck: Michel's passport goes missing, making it impossible for him to return to France. So he stays in Moscow. In the meantime, a Party cell has installed itself in another old factory. They send a delegation to Lenin to request permission to resume perfume production – and they remember the Frenchman, who is able to start working again. He could leave the country now if he wanted, but he decides to stay. The Soviet authorities offer him a salary in hard currency, trips to spas, opportunities to travel abroad, but he gets down to work in what is now one of the largest perfume factories in the world.

In keeping with the new general line, the Soviet power extends new offers to old bourgeois experts. While they had been victims of cultural-revolutionary 'specialist baiting' during the First Five-Year Plan (1928–32), they are now considered valuable examples of the Soviet state's successful deployment of the old intelligentsia.

Michel sets to work designing wooden models for perfume bottles, based on the creations of Lalique, Houbigant and Coty. The new society of labourers and farmers must be made to understand that specialists, even those from the ranks of the old intelligentsia, are as essential as a perfumer's nose is to his profession. Master Michel is given his own laboratory, and even students, so that he can pass on his knowledge. The proletarian state is now prepared to grant privileges to bourgeois specialists – including houses, trips to health resorts, cars and, above all, an increase in social prestige.

And on the eve of the twentieth anniversary of the October Revolution, Auguste Michel – bourgeois expert and product of a bygone world – is assigned an important new task. He is to create a perfume worthy of the latest superlative the Soviet Union has to offer, a perfume named Palace of Soviets, with an aroma that adequately expresses this masterpiece of engineering. A perfume of superlatives, of the new age, of technical innovation, a perfume that goes beyond the scent of violets, tuberose and hyacinth. But what does a feat of technical engineering smell like? What fragrance would encapsulate the era of Stalin? Michel hesitates, sceptical that a perfume smelling of cement, steel and mortar will find an audience, but he accepts the commission and gets to work. It would be a perfume in keeping with the times, commensurate with the tallest structure in the world, the Palace of Soviets, parliament of the new classless society, a monumental sculpture that would reach into the Moscow sky, its 420-metre tower likely to be lost in the clouds.

Dozens of architects had taken part in the design competition, including Le Corbusier, Erich Mendelsohn, Walter Gropius and the Vesnin brothers. The winner was expected to build a structure more impressive than the Empire State Building in New York or the Palace of Nations in Geneva. The Palace of Soviets would be

11   Model of the Palace of Soviets by Boris Iofan

more than just a monumental building, it would be a
symbol, erected on the site of the Cathedral of Christ the
Saviour, the largest Neo-Byzantine Russian Orthodox
church in the centre of Moscow. The cathedral had been

demolished in 1932 and now, in 1937, construction of the building based on Boris Iofan's design was in full swing. Twenty years after the October Revolution, the Soviet state was cooking up new triumphs: the tallest building in the world, and the ultimate fragrance for the new epoch, the Palace of Soviets perfume. But while the model of Iofan's tower was a much-admired attraction in the Soviet pavilion at the Paris world expo in 1937, the perfume never materialized.[3]

The artistic council that passed judgement on Michel's creation felt that the 'perfume of construction' was not a success. The council instead chose a composition named something like '1 May', but it was not well received by the public. Loskutov complains to Michel that the council members were hypocritical guardians of morals who rejected successful perfumes like 'Carmen' just because the name reminded them of gambling dens or loose women. In Loskutov's eyes, the council members were nothing but 'Tartuffes who rename meatballs instead of improving them', and they would have done better to dispense with pompous-sounding perfumes like '1 May' and stick with the good old flowery fragrances instead. Michel agrees: 'That's right. I'm grateful to you, the Frenchman said, clasping my hand. And then he told me about many of the things that upset him both in his professional life as a perfumer and personally.' Michel says that L'Origan and Coty have long been out of fashion, but people in the Soviet Union had not grasped that yet. A bottle of Chanel perfume cost 5,000 francs in Paris, which was naturally ridiculous. Michel mentions the tremendous growth in fragrance production in the Soviet Union, but also claims that it is not nearly enough. And he calls for a major initiative to produce fragrances and the establishment of a huge perfume factory in Tula – a 'Dneprostroi of scents' comparable to the massive dam and power station that had recently been built on the Dnieper River.[4]

Auguste Michel, the expert from the age of the *ancien régime* who stayed behind in the chaos of the Russian Civil War, who came to terms with his situation and contributed to the revival of the perfume industry, was now benefitting from the late rehabilitation of the culture of perfume and cosmetics, which had been categorically branded as bourgeois in the post-revolutionary years. The social climbers who streamed to the cities in the age of industrialization and formed a kind of new middle class could afford the cosmetics, perfumes and clothing now being produced on the basis of the planned economy, for large numbers of customers.

And, indeed, diplomats' wives and foreign visitors were amazed by how much the Moscow fashion scene had changed in the mid-1930s. The shop windows and *ateliers* reminded them of those in Paris or New York. They saw fashions that could easily have been featured in the West – but these fashions were found only in the shop windows, not in everyday life. The image of the Soviet woman had changed as well. Women were to be seen as mothers and protectors of the flock, and to enjoy without guilt the luxury to which they were entitled – including all of the jewellery, accessories and dresses advertised in the Soviet fashion magazines of the time, with names like *The Art of Dressing* and *Atelier*. It was not simplicity and modesty that were called for, but rather 'grandness, classicism, uniqueness and preciousness'.[5]

The Italian-French fashion designer Elsa Schiaparelli was bewildered by the 'orgy of chiffon' and fur-lined dresses she saw in Moscow, and her advice that clothing should be 'simple and practical' fell on deaf ears. Something fundamental had changed, as indicated by the many fashion shows, posters and advertisements, and particularly by the House of Prototypes that opened in Moscow in 1935. This institution was expected to solve the paradoxical problem of taking a highly sophisticated product, essentially dependent on complex artisanal craftsmanship, and mass producing it in a process based on simplification, standardization and price reduction. It had to resolve the contradiction between the unpredictability of fashion, which develops almost subconsciously through moods and feelings, and the need to follow a production plan that had been defined in advance. Fashion – including perfume – was no longer the spontaneous and unforeseeable anticipation of 'what is coming' (Walter Benjamin), but rather the implementation of a concept with long-term validity based on a scientific approach, not the anarchy of the market. The planned economy contradicted fashion as a process:

> The powerful bureaucracy established under Stalinism that governed the industry through a rigid, hierarchically structured and overcentralized system determined the functioning of the field of fashion up to the end of socialism. With their activities informed by the hierarchical principle, socialist state textile factories did not respond to the desires of their customers but to the desires of their superiors, from whom they received both supplies and orders to fulfil their plan.[6]

Queuing outside textile and clothing shops was part of the lifelong reality of Soviet citizens, just as much as their lifelong confrontation with the irrationality of a system that was inelastic and inflexible, that had overridden the back-and-forth of supply and demand and pulled off the feat of offering summer clothing in winter, winter clothing in summer, and perfumes that no one wanted – entirely in accordance with and in thrall to the economic plan.

Perfume production was also restructured to fit the planned economy. In keeping with the pathos of the Five-Year Plan – and in the words of Auguste Michel – the perfume industry was to become a powerhouse like Dneprostroi, Europe's largest hydroelectric station, which had been built between 1927 and 1932. Michel had founded a 'Soviet school of perfume' whose students shaped the industry after him: Pavel Ivanov and Alexei Pogudkin. In his own time, Walter Benjamin had pondered whether tethering fashion to an economic plan might increase the tonnes of clothing produced and the number of consumers purchasing it, but at a high price – namely, the death of fashion as the most sensitive expression of social moods, the anticipation of 'what is coming': 'Does fashion die (as in Russia, for example) because it can no longer keep up the tempo – at least in certain fields?'[7]

We do not know what happened to Auguste Michel in 1937. All trace of him is lost, leaving only speculation. Maybe he continued living in the Soviet Union under a different name, perhaps because he had married a Soviet citizen; maybe he moved out of Moscow and was swallowed up by the anonymity of the vast country. But his disappearance is probably connected to the repressive measures of the *Yezhovshchina*, or Great Purge. Michel was a foreigner, with both Soviet and French citizenship. He was a foreign specialist who could easily have been implicated and tried as a spy, saboteur or agent. And he was a member of the bourgeoisie, and involved in the production of luxuries to boot – and for that reason alone he was doomed. It is also not clear what happened to Andrei Yevseyev, Michel's co-producer, the designer who had moved with him from Brocard to Novaya Zarya.

We do know the fate of Mikhail Loskutov, however – the writer who interviewed Auguste Michel. Loskutov – born in 1902 in Kursk and a member of the Soviet writers' association – was a talented young author, according to Konstantin Paustovsky. His last known residence was in Moscow, at 3 Karetny Pereulok, flat 2. He was arrested on 12 January 1940 and sentenced to death by the Military Collegium of the Supreme Court for 'participation in the counter-revolutionary activity of a terrorist organization'. Loskutov was shot on 28 July 1941, shortly after Germany invaded the Soviet Union, when the Soviet state security forces of the NKVD had begun killing many prisoners as the Wehrmacht drew near.[8]

A panorama of Soviet life was on display in the Soviet pavilion at the Paris world expo in 1937, including design, fashion, accessories and cosmetics. Dignitaries from the world of Soviet design and perfume attended the expo as well. Auguste Michel could easily have encountered Ernest Beaux, who certainly visited the spectacular exhibition, along with everyone else who had anything to do with the Russian scene in France. Even the heirs to Diaghilev's dance troupe appear in the programme of events at the exhibition grounds near the Eiffel Tower. The model of the 420-metre-high Palace of Soviets was one of the biggest attractions at the fair. But there was no fragrance to go with it. Instead, in 1939, the perfume known as Red Moscow was awarded the grand prize at the All-Union Exhibition of Light Industry in the new fairgrounds of the Exhibition of Achievements of the National Economy (VDNKh) in Moscow. The advertising poster designed by Alexei Volter shows a monumental perfume bottle integrated into the silhouette of the Kremlin towers, as if depicting the perfect fusion of fragrance and the centre of power.

The seductive scent of power: Coco Chanel and Polina Zhemchuzhina-Molotova – two careers in the twentieth century

A historic event – the Russian Revolution – led the pre-revolutionary Bouquet de Catherine to become Chanel No. 5 and Red Moscow. This bifurcated development was embodied by the life trajectories of the perfumers Ernest Beaux (Paris) and Auguste Michel (Moscow), and it materialized in the different production lines of a private company named Chanel and a Soviet state trust named TeZhe. Both perfumes represented the desire for beauty in times of war and deprivation, as well as the break with a world whose time had passed.

Even perfumes are not immune to the violence and seductions of their epoch. The time has now come to explore the connection between the world of fragrance and the aura of power.[1] The existence of this connection does not need to be asserted, merely revealed.

Though we do not know everything about Coco Chanel and her world, we know a great deal. But what do we know about the world filled with the scents produced by Novaya Zarya, and particularly the

12 Polina Zhemchuzhina at her desk

company's most popular fragrance, Krasnaya Moskva – Red Moscow? Coco Chanel was too famous and too important to be ignored. Polina Zhemchuzhina-Molotova is known mostly for being the wife of Soviet Foreign Minister Molotov, and for being exiled for five years under Stalin. What many do not realize, however, is that she also played a major role in the development of the Soviet perfume and cosmetics industry.[2]

Gabrielle Chanel was born on 19 August 1883 and grew up in rural France. She came into contact with high society early on, not because she had political ambitions, but because she was pulled into the orbit of power as a partner to rich and influential men.[3] In the eyes of these men she was an accessory, but in reality she was a woman who never relinquished her self-will or independence. If anything, she made use of the men, if for no other reason than that their lives and experiences were a never-ending lesson in a social milieu inherently alien to her, and she wanted to absorb every possible aspect of cosmopolitanism. As the beautiful, witty, sarcastic and extremely well-read woman at her lovers' side, she unexpectedly made the acquaintance of powerful people and learned to navigate their universe – in the hunting parties of Étienne Balsan at Chateau de Royallieu near Compiègne, and as the companion to the English dandy Boy Capel, who was friendly with Clemenceau and with whom she inhabited the chic worlds of Deauville, Biarritz and Paris, where she also met the richest man in Britain at the time, the Duke of Westminster (nicknamed 'Bendor').

She circulated through the houses of the English aristocracy for many years, and shuttled back and forth between Paris and her home in Mayfair. There are many photographs of her with Winston Churchill, who admired her and with whom she remained in close and fateful contact. Samuel Goldwyn brought her to Los Angeles, where she dressed the stars of Hollywood and studied the workings of the market of modern mass consumption. As a prominent fashion designer, she entertained nobles such as the Prince of Wales – the future Edward VIII – with whom she was on a first-name basis ('David'). She housed a Romanov in her villa and shared not only intimacy with him, but also his reactionary world view. Officially, she was an apolitical style icon, but she held distinct views in her social circles between the wars, particularly in the unsettled period of the Popular Front government. When her seamstresses went on strike for higher pay under the Popular Front, she took it as a personal breach of trust, and she retaliated when the war broke out by closing her shops and turning her employees out into the street.

Her co-operation with the Germans during the occupation from 1940 to 1944 – now seen as a scandal – was, in her eyes, just the continuation of what she had always done as someone who considered herself independent and uninterested in politics. She perceived the French defeat and German occupation of Paris to be a calamity, but she went about her business nonetheless,

13 Gabrielle Chanel in a sailor top with her dog

simply under different circumstances.[4] She continued
to live in her suite at the Ritz on the Place Vendôme, a
hotel that now served as the finest accommodation for
senior German occupation officials and prominent visitors from the Reich. She dined, as always, on exquisite
dishes concocted despite the war shortages, side by side
in the dining room with Nazi personnel. And she had

an elegant and handsome lover, only this time he was German: Baron Hans Günther von Dincklage, whom she had known prior to the occupation. He now worked for the intelligence and security apparatus of the 'Third Reich' in France, as the special attaché at the German embassy, where he was responsible for espionage and propaganda. She took part in the lively German–French social scene with its private art viewings, gala dinners and receptions. In an attempt to free her nephew, who had been deported to the Reich for forced labour, she made two trips to Berlin and offered to establish contact with leadership circles in Great Britain, specifically with an old friend who had since become prime minister of the United Kingdom and Hitler's fiercest opponent: Winston Churchill. The purpose of this contact would have been to sound out the possibility, in the waning days of the Reich, of forging a separate peace between Germany and Britain and shifting the focus of the war to Bolshevism. Chanel met with Walter Schellenberg from the Reich Main Security Office in Berlin and was put up in the guesthouse of the villa built for Ernst Marlier by the architect Paul Baumgarten on the Wannsee – the site that would play such a momentous role in the 'final solution to the Jewish question'.

Her collaboration with the Germans is not just a rumour; evidence of it can be found in witness statements by members of the Résistance, the case files of French courts after the liberation of Paris, and the documents of the German authorities.[5] What the documents do not tell us is whether her activities ever caused anyone great personal harm. The more grievous fault, perhaps, was that such tacit, ordinary, everyday cohabitation and collaboration gave a veneer of normality to an occupying force that brutally supressed all resistance and, with the support of the Vichy government, sent tens of thousands of French Jews to their death. Life in the metropolis thus seemed simply to carry on

as before, only with slightly different protagonists –
above all, the cultivated Germans who spoke fluent
French, had a lifelong fascination with France and
could not imagine a Europe without French culture.
They included writers and admirers of France with an
excellent knowledge of the country, the type of people
only rarely found in the Eastern European cities occupied by the Nazis. There were people from the embassy
who knew their way around: Otto Abetz, and indeed
Hans Günther von Dincklage; well-known authors such
as Friedrich Sieburg, who wrote *Gott in Frankreich*
('Is God a Frenchman?') in 1929 to convey something
of the magic of French culture to the Germans; the
sculptor Arno Breker, who kept an *atelier* in Paris and
accompanied Hitler through the early-morning streets
of the city during the Führer's visit on 23 June 1940,
and who also took up residence during the occupation
in an 'Aryanized' building on the Île Saint-Louis that
belonged to Helena Rubinstein, inventor of the beauty
salon and founder of a globally successful cosmetics
company.[6]

The fact that prominent figures in Parisian society
'went along with' the occupation was an invaluable
boost to the prestige of the German leadership. And
they did so not just because they were under pressure;
individuals such as Jean Cocteau and Serge Lifar made
no secret of their admiration for the handsome men in
black uniforms, and they were incapable of helping one
of their old companions, Max Jacob, when he faced
mortal danger. Jacob died in the Drancy internment
camp, and his siblings were murdered in Auschwitz.[7]

Paris, the city that had captured the imagination
of cultivated Germans, the very measure of elegance,
was now occupied by German soldiers and intelligence
experts. The Champs-Élysées was a victory parade
ground, and the Führer was photographed against the
backdrop of the Eiffel Tower in the early morning by

cameras intent on capturing the moment of triumph and humiliation in the empty streets. The city that was once a haven for Russian Civil War refugees and then a refuge for German oppositionists of every stripe and profession – Jews, communists, socialists and the bourgeoisie who no longer felt safe back home – had now become a nightmare for them, but a dreamland for the ordinary German soldiers lucky enough not to be deployed to the Eastern Front.[8]

In France, or at least in Paris, it was possible to find what had long ceased to exist in the Reich: a cosmopolitan life with cafés, cinemas and shops, wine, cheese – and perfume. Perfume was perhaps the most French of all souvenirs that soldiers could send to their sweethearts back home; the bottles were compact and convenient, and Parisian fragrances dazzled in German provincial towns, a reminder of the wider world during long nights of bombing. No wonder German soldiers flocked to 31 rue Cambon to stock up on perfumes from the Chanel boutique.

The occupation also gave Chanel the opportunity to settle a long-held score. A contract from 1924 had transferred most of the production and sales rights for Chanel No. 5 to the company owned by the brothers Pierre and Paul Wertheimer – a contract that made the perfume a tremendous success even outside of France, particularly in the USA. Coco Chanel was convinced that she had been swindled in the negotiations, and she sought (unsuccessfully) to have the contract revised. The German occupation finally gave her the chance to take action against the Wertheimer brothers and try to get her hands on part of the perfume business – a French form of 'Aryanization'. To do so, she made use of her connections with lawyers and politicians serving the Vichy regime. Chanel had never concealed her animosity towards Jews. She did not like Jews – perhaps because she had been raised that way by the Sisters of the Holy Cross; perhaps because her relationships with Russian monarchist emigrants led her to associate Jews with Bolshevism; perhaps because she believed that her business partners, who were Jewish, had deceived her. This was despite the fact that the new sales methods introduced by Pierre and Paul Wertheimer had turned Chanel No. 5 into a global sensation. A bottle of Chanel No. 5 was even placed in the foundations of the cosmetics pavilion at the New York World's Fair in 1939, the theme of which was 'The World of Tomorrow' – held on the eve of World War II.[9]

Chanel must have known what was in store for her when the Americans and Charles de Gaulle's forces moved into Paris. Thousands of girls and women who had taken up with Germans were accused of 'collaboration horizontale' and driven through the streets in humiliation – but not Coco Chanel, who was arrested at the Ritz and only briefly questioned by the Commission d'Épuration. In a strange irony of history, it was apparently a letter from Winston Churchill that spared her from being put on trial. Chanel fled to Switzerland until the situation calmed down. She even rekindled her German connections there, with both Günther von Dincklage and Walter Schellenberg. And she prepared to return to the Paris stage, where she would celebrate her comeback in the mid-1950s.[10]

When it comes to the life and fate of Polina Zhemchuzhina-Molotova, we must look somewhat further afield, as there is barely any trace of her in the awareness or memory of those in the West. The biography of this remarkable woman has yet to be written.[11] In the Soviet Union, many people at least knew her name and her fate, and that she was associated with something spectacular. And Soviet Jews knew that she was a special case. Although married to Vyacheslav Molotov, the second most powerful man in the country after Stalin, she was arrested and convicted in 1949 on the pretext of having ties to Zionist circles. She spent five years in exile and, immediately after Stalin died, she was released on the order of Lavrentiy Beria, head of the secret police.

But she was not just the wife of a prominent Soviet Party functionary and statesman – her name is also associated with the establishment of the Soviet cosmetics and perfume industry. She is additionally said to have been responsible for the fact that the bottle for Krasnaya Moskva, the most popular of all Soviet perfumes, was given a stopper resembling the onion domes of the Kremlin.[12]

Polina Zhemchuzhina came from the impoverished environs of the Jewish shtetl. She was born on 28 February 1897 to the tailor Solomon Karpovsky in the settlement of Polohy in the Yekaterinoslav Governate, now the Zaporozhia region of Ukraine. From 1910 she worked in a tobacco factory in the city of Yekaterinoslav (now Dnipro), which was a hub of industrialization, rail transport and banking in the southern Russian Empire – and, with a population that was 40 per cent Jewish, was also one of the most important centres of Jewish life in what was known as the Pale of Settlement. When the Russian Revolution began in 1917, she was employed as a cashier in a pharmacy. She stayed in the country during the revolution and civil war years, while her sister and brother emigrated to the British Mandate of Palestine in 1918. Her brother later moved to the USA, where he became a successful businessman by the name of Sam Carp and helped the Soviet government to establish trade relations, purchase warships and acquire military equipment through his Car Export and Import Corporation. Polina corresponded with her sister in Palestine until 1939.

Pulling together the scattered details about her reveals the following image: when she was interrogated after her arrest in 1949 and reproached for having changed her

name, she explained that she had simply translated *Perl*,
the Yiddish for 'pearl', into Russian, *Zhemchuzhina*,
which was common practice at the time. She joined
the Red Army and Bolshevik Party in 1918, where she
served as a political education and propaganda commissar, and she ran a club. In 1919, she was sent to Kiev to
work underground, and later in Kharkov she was issued
identity documents in the name of Polina Semyonovna
Zhemchuzhina, which enabled her to continue her
underground work in Ukraine. Zhemchuzhina was a
women's work instructor in the Central Committee of
the Communist Party of Ukraine from 1919 to 1920,
then ran the women's department of the Zaporizhia
City Committee from 1920 to 1921, and worked as
an instructor for the Rogozhsko-Simonovsky District
Committee of the Bolshevik Party in Moscow from
1921 to 1922.

All of this speaks of a young woman who was decisive
in the confusion of the Civil War and was particularly
committed to the cause of women, living in a part of
the empire that had been overrun multiple times by
the shifting front lines of the Reds and Whites, where
horrific pogroms had taken place against Jews, mostly
carried out by the Whites. Emigrating to Palestine or
America or throwing oneself into the fight for political power were obvious options at the time, as Yuri
Slezkine points out in his book on *The Jewish Century*.
Zhemchuzhina allied herself with the Bolsheviks long
before their victory was assured, a decision that was not
without risk to her own life.

In the course of her activities for women's affairs,
she attended a congress where she apparently caught
the eye of a prominent Bolshevik: Vyacheslav Molotov,
whom she married in 1921. This automatically placed
her in the inner circle of power. She and her husband
lived with Stalin and his wife in a kind of communal
apartment, and it took some time before they were able

to move into their own flat – just across the hall. Polina was close friends with Stalin's second wife, Nadezhda, a woman who was also politically active and had a mind of her own. Nadezhda was publicly berated by Stalin at a celebratory dinner one evening, prompting her to storm out of the dining room; she shot herself with her revolver later that night. Stalin's daughter Svetlana Alliluyeva – who met Polina Zhemchuzhina in Moscow when the latter returned from exile in Kustanai in Kazakhstan in the 1950s – recounts in her memoirs what had befallen Nadezhda Alliluyeva shortly before her suicide: 'Polina Molotov had been at the banquet with my mother and the others. All of them witnessed the quarrel and my mother's departure, but no one gave it much importance. Polina Molotov left the banquet with my mother so she wouldn't be alone. They went out and walked around the Kremlin Palace several times until my mother calmed down.'[13] After the suicide, Polina was one of the first called to the deathbed of Stalin's wife.

In the 1920s, Zhemchuzhina was apparently determined to continue her professional education, first at the Workers' Faculty of the Second Moscow State University (1923), then at the First Moscow State University (1925), and finally at the Faculty of Economics of the Plekhanov Moscow Institute of the National Economy (1925–6). She held management positions very early on, as secretary of the Party cell at the Novaya Zarya perfume factory (1927–9) and then as director of the factory itself (1930–2). From 1932 to 1936, she was head of the state perfumery trust, TeZhe. This was followed by executive positions in the People's Commissariat for the Food Industry. From July 1936, she managed the Main Department of the Perfume, Cosmetics, Synthetics and Soap Industry, and from November 1937 she was Deputy People's Commissar for the Food Industry of the USSR.

On 19 January 1939, the People's Commissariat for the Fishing Industry was spun off from the People's Commissariat for the Food Industry, and the person appointed to lead it was Polina Zhemchuzhina – the first and only woman to serve as people's commissar in the history of the Soviet Union. Stalin himself is said to have chosen her for the position, even though her husband was against it, as Molotov later claimed in a conversation with Felix Chuev.[14] In March 1939, Zhemchuzhina was elected as a candidate to the Central Committee of the Communist Party, giving her access to the inner circle of power in the year of the 18th Party Congress, which was supposed to mark the end of the *Yezhovschina* (the purges of 1937–8), and at which important foreign policy decisions were announced. It was at this congress that Stalin held his 'chestnut speech', declaring that, after the capitulation of the Western powers at the Munich Conference of 1938 and the failure to establish a collective security system with England and France, he was not prepared to 'pull chestnuts out of the fire' for others, by which he meant waging war alone against Nazi Germany. And on 10 August 1939, the Politburo of the Central Committee of the Communist Party resolved to review all of the materials pertaining to Zhemchuzhina.

In November 1939, Zhemchuzhina was unexpectedly removed from her post as People's Commissar for the Fishing Industry and was assigned to lead the Department for Textiles and Haberdashery in the People's Commissariat for Light Industry of the Russian Soviet Federative Socialist Republic (RSFSR). In February 1941, at the 18th All-Union Conference of the Communist Party, she was additionally removed from her position as a candidate for the Central Committee, a visible loss of status that was essentially a demotion. From October 1946 to 1948, she served as head of the Main Haberdashery Office in what had become the Ministry of Light Industry of the USSR, and she was subsequently a member of the reserve staff of the Ministry of Light Industry of the RSFSR until her arrest on 26 January 1949. On 29 December 1949, she was sentenced to five years in exile. She was arrested again on 21 January 1953, but was released from custody on 23 March and rehabilitated two days later by resolution of a special session of the Ministry of Internal Affairs. She retired the same year.

Something must have happened in 1938–9 that resulted in Zhemchuzhina's removal from the inner circle of leadership – something that was not openly addressed but seems to have played a significant role ten years later, as far as we can tell today. Perhaps it was her connections with people abroad and foreigners in the Soviet Union – meaning, on the one hand, her ongoing communication with her brother in the USA and sister in Palestine, and, on the other hand, the close social relations she must have entertained with members of the diplomatic corps, and particularly with Marjorie Davies, wife of the American ambassador in Moscow, Joseph Davies.[15]

Like many diplomats and their spouses, Marjorie Davies haunted the antiques shops, markets and bazaars of the capital, which were brimming with the dispersed riches of an aristocracy that had been dispossessed, decimated and scattered around the world. You could still find Netherlandish paintings, Meissen and Sèvres porcelain, Roentgen furniture and valuable furs there, and it is not out of the question that friendly social ties could lead to the provision of help in acquiring such objects of desire. And against the backdrop of the purges and general 'spy mania', such otherwise harmless-seeming relationships could become a deadly threat. Simply maintaining contact with family members abroad, even if they had left the country before the revolution, was very risky.[16] Under these conditions, the most basic social interactions were regarded with a suspicion that even Polina Zhemchuzhina was apparently unable to avoid. The receptions at the American embassy in Spasso House were renowned for their opulence; they brought together *tout-Moscou* and were mentioned in both the memoirs of diplomats such as George F. Kennan and works of literature such as Mikhail Bulgakov's *The Master and Margarita*. American ambassador Joseph Davies provides an admiring account of the acquaintanceship with 'Madame Molotov', who invited his wife Marjorie to a 'ladies' luncheon' at the Molotovs' dacha:

> Marjorie went to Madame Molotov's luncheon. It was quite extraordinary – a group of wives of the commissars all of whom are actively engaged as engineers, doctors, or factory managers.
>
> Madame Molotov, wife of the Premier, is a Member of Cabinet and has been Commissar for Fisheries and is now Commissar for Cosmetics. She is a very extraordinary woman. The manner in which she has established these very chic perfume shops and cosmetic beauty parlours indicates a great deal of executive direction. She and the rest of these serious-minded women who are engineers, physicians, etc., found great interest in Marjorie, particularly in the fact that a woman of her type should be so much interested in serious business matters and should herself be 'a working-woman.' This idea of having a 'hen luncheon' is something most novel in Soviet experience, as I am advised.[17]

The ambassador's wife herself was also impressed by 'Madame Molotov':

> The day we went through the factory (one of four she runs) making fine perfumes, creams, etc., Mme Molotov asked us to lunch with her. We accepted with pleasure. . . . The day arrived and off we went – an hour in the country out Rublova Woods way – past several

large villas, and finally the green fence and guards came into view. Gate was open, and en route to house we saw many more guards.

House modern, large (but by no means a palace in or out), rather plain. Good taste – ample, but not furnished in a cosy or 'lived-in' manner, though in every way adequate. Entrance hall, big stairs, dressing rooms, etc. Living room spacious. No photos or bric-a-brac. Dining room large with huge casement windows. Table decorated in cyclamen – at least 3" each. Standing on floor around room were eight or ten potted lilacs – white and lavender – fine big heads and full of flowers.

Also present were the wife of Embassy Secretary George F. Kennan, Marjorie Davies's own secretary Edith Wells, and the wives of prominent Soviet functionaries who would soon disappear in the purges, such as Vlas Chubar, Nikolai Krestinsky and Boris Stomonyakov. The lunch was a very refined multi-course affair.[18] Later, on 10 September 1938, Joseph Davies wrote to Molotov himself, addressing his letter to the 'Dear Mr. Premier':

My stay in Russia I shall always remember with keen appreciation of the universal kindness I received at the hands of the fine Russian people, and the many courtesies and kindnesses tendered to me by the representatives of the government of the Soviet Union.

Under separate cover I have forwarded to you an autographed copy of the catalogue of my collection of Russian pictures which, with the aid of your government, I was able to secure to present to my old alma mater, the University of Wisconsin.[19]

Polina turns up in other places as well, where the *nomenklatura* members carried on their sophisticated social lives: at the Molotovs' dacha near Sosny on the banks of the Moskva River, where she can be seen in photos with her daughter, swimming and weaving a wreath of water lilies, and where Molotov and the writer Alexander Arosev – probably the most important Soviet cultural diplomat, who was arrested in 1938 and murdered – splashed in the water like little boys and held deep, erudite discussions about literature and art.[20]

Things that were commonplace in normal times, such as regular contact with the USA, became perilous offences in the years of the purges. In 1935–6, contact between the Soviet Union and the United States was still extremely close. This was the high point of 'Soviet Americanism' (Hans Rogger). Soviet delegations were sent to the 'New World', which had become a more important point of orientation than the 'Old World' of Europe. Engineers studied the construction of hydro-electric plants and skyscrapers, and architects visited the biggest building site of the New Deal, Rockefeller Center in New York. The most popular authors in the Soviet Union, Ilya Ilf and Yevgeny Petrov, toured the USA and published accounts of their travels through 'Little Golden America' in major newspapers and glossy magazines back home. Anastas Mikoyan took a large delegation to the USA to study the canning industry, food production, Fordism in the slaughterhouses of Chicago, and the workings of automats and fast-food restaurants. And at the 1939 World's Fair in New York, the Soviet Union still had a spectacular pavilion.[21]

But 1939 brought about a rupture in Polina Zhemchuzhina's career. In June, the directors of the perfume industry trust (Glavparfyumerprom) who worked with Zhemchuzhina, the dermatologist Ilya Belakhov, a man named Sliosberg who was head of the trust for food, fragrances and oils (Glavpishchearomatmaslo), and the sisters Yulika and Nadezhda Kanel, who were doctors, were arrested and tortured into signing pre-formulated confessions in what was known as the

'Snakepit'. Before he was shot, Belakhov stated for the record: 'They hit me and demanded that I confess to having lived with Comrade Zhemchuzhina and being a spy. I could not slander the woman, as this is a lie and I have been impotent from birth.' Bogdan Kobulov, who conducted the interrogations at the behest of Beria, later admitted that he had personally beaten Belakhov:[22] 'The aim was to get confessions about hostile activities and the nature of the relationship with a family member of one of the leaders of the Party and government, in accordance with Beria's orders.'

On 10 August 1939, the Politburo adopted a resolution 'regarding Com. Zhemchuzhina':

> 1. It has been determined that Com. Zh. was imprudent in her associations and, as a result, several hostile espionage elements found their way into the orbit of Com. Zh., who unintentionally facilitated their espionage activities. 2. It has been determined that all of the materials pertaining to Com. Zhemchuzhina will be carefully reviewed. 3. Com. Zhemchuzhina is to be relieved from her post as People's Commissar for the Fisheries Industry. These measures are to be carried out sequentially.

On 21 November 1939, Zhemchuzhina was confirmed as head of the Department for Textiles and Haberdashery in the People's Commissariat for Light Industry of the RSFSR, which was essentially a demotion from the union level to the republic level.[23] The next step was taken at a plenary session of the Central Committee on the eve of the 18th Party Conference in early 1941, at which a number of prominent candidates were withdrawn, including former Commissar of Foreign Affairs Maxim Litvinov and Polina Zhemchuzhina.

Zhemchuzhina's appearance at the meeting left a lasting impression on Georgi Dimitrov. On 20 February 1941, he wrote in his diary:

What happened to Zhemchuzhina was especially strik-
ing. (She made a good speech. 'The party rewarded me,
gave me encouragement for good work. But I let things
get out of hand; my deputy (as people's commissar of
the fishing industry) turned out to be a spy, so did a
woman friend. I failed to demonstrate element[ary] vigi-
lance. I drew a lesson from all that. I declare that I will
work to the end of my days honestly, like a Bolshevik
. . .') During voting, one member abstained (Molotov).
Perhaps because he is her husband; even so, that was
hardly correct.

Khrushchev also recalled Zhemchuzhina's appearance
and the criticism levelled against Molotov by many
Central Committee members, who complained that his
abstention indicated he had put his personal concerns as
a husband before Party discipline.[24]

As Oleg Khlevniuk and Stephen Kotkin interpret
the situation, on 10 August 1939 Stalin had permitted
accusations to be aired against the 'enemy spy elements'
around Zhemchuzhina, but he did nothing more than
demote her. Both Kotkin and Khlevniuk view this as
a warning shot directed at Zhemchuzhina's husband,
Molotov.[25] Nonetheless, it is obvious that, in the tense,
hyper-nervous years of the Great Purge, Zhemchuzhina's
American connections could prove to be disastrous and
were ultimately behind her demotion in 1939. This
incident would play a role again later on, when Polina
Zhemchuzhina was arrested in 1949. But at the New
Year's reception in the Kremlin in 1939, Zhemchuzhina
and Molotov were still seated next to Stalin.

After Germany invaded the Soviet Union, and then
throughout the war, Polina Zhemchuzhina was one
of the most prominent members of the Jewish Anti-
Fascist Committee, which campaigned worldwide (but
especially in the USA) to promote Jewish solidarity and
mobilize support for the USSR in its fight against Hitler.

Zhemchuzhina thus became a point of contact between the Soviet world and the Western anti-Hitler coalition. The chairman of the organization was Solomon Mikhoels, a well-known actor and director of the Moscow State Jewish Theatre, who was highly respected and even beloved by Soviet Jews. Zhemchuzhina's trial records include a letter from Mikhoels, in which he requests her support for a sick colleague. She was apparently so fearless that she was still writing letters to her brother in the USA in 1946.[26] The Jewish Anti-Fascist Committee gained renown through a book compiled by Ilya Ehrenburg and Vasily Grossman, known in English as *The Black Book* (subtitled *The Criminal Mass Murder of Jews by Fascist German Invaders in the Temporarily Occupied Regions of the Soviet Union and in the Fascist Extermination Camps of Poland during the War 1941–1945*) – though the book was pulled from circulation shortly after it was completed and could not be published in Russia until the end of the Soviet Union.[27]

On the thirty-first anniversary of the October Revolution in 1948, there was, as always, a reception in the Kremlin, hosted by Molotov for accredited diplomats in Moscow. Zhemchuzhina made a point of talking to the newly appointed Israeli ambassador, Golda Meir, who had received an enthusiastic welcome by tens of thousands of Jews when she visited the Choral Synagogue after arriving in Moscow. Golda Meir, who was aware of the major role played by the Soviet Union in the founding of the State of Israel, but also of the repression of Jews in the Soviet Union, described her encounter with Polina Zhemchuzhina, who came up to greet her:

'I am so pleased to meet you, at last,' she said with real warmth and even excitement. Then she added, 'I speak Yiddish, you know.'

'Are you Jewish?' I asked in some surprise.

'Yes,' she said, answering me in Yiddish, '*Ich bin a yiddishe tochter.*' (I am a daughter of the Jewish people.) We talked together for quite a long time. She knew all about the events at the synagogue and told me how good it was that we had gone. 'The Jews wanted so much to see you,' she said.

In the course of the conversation, Zhemchuzhina remarked critically on the principle of collective ownership in the kibbutz:

'That's not a good idea,' she said. 'People don't like sharing everything. Even Stalin is against that. You should acquaint yourself with Stalin's thoughts and writings on the subject.' Before she returned to her other guests, she put her arm around Sarah [Golda Meir's daughter] and, with tears in her eyes, said, 'Be well. If everything goes well with you, it will go well for all Jews everywhere.'[28]

On 29 December 1948, 'Madame Molotov' was expelled from the Party, and on 29 January 1949, she was arrested. She was accused of having had 'a criminal connection to Jewish nationalists over the course of many years'. Two months later, her husband was dismissed from his position as foreign minister, thus losing a great deal of his influence with 'Stalin's team' (Sheila Fitzpatrick). Several of Zhemchuzhina's relatives were also arrested: her brother A. S. Karpovsky, her sister R. S. Leshnyavskaya, and her nephews I. I. Shteinberg, director of Plant No. 339 in the Ministry of the Aviation Industry, and S. M. Golovanevsky, assistant to the head of the Main Directorate of the Forestry Industry in the Ministry of the Fishing Industry. Karpovsky and Leshnyavskaya 'did not withstand the regime applied to them' (meaning torture) and died in prison.[29]

On 29 December 1949, Zhemchuzhina was sentenced by a special session of the Ministry of State Security

(MGB) of the USSR to five years in exile in Kustanai, east of the Urals. She was arrested again in Kustanai in January 1953 and taken to Moscow in preparation for a show trial. According to her case file, she remarked: 'If that is what the government has decided, then so be it.'

When she was interrogated, she denied every allegation. The authorities wanted to prove that Zhemchuzhina had supported an idea proposed by Mikhoels and others, to create a 'Jewish California in Crimea', and that she had concealed a Zionist anti-Soviet conspiracy. No charge was considered too absurd to hold against her. One of her subordinates even accused her of having tried to seduce him. Another claimed to have seen her in the Moscow Choral Synagogue, sitting downstairs in a place generally reserved for men instead of in the usual seats for women upstairs in the gallery. She rejected the allegation that she had spread a rumour about Mikhoels having been murdered – contrary to the official line that he had died in a 'traffic accident'. And she remained adamant that she had never been part of a Zionist conspiracy.[30]

When Lavrentiy Beria sought her out on 10 March 1953, five days after Stalin's death and one day after his funeral, to tell her that she was free, the first thing she asked was how Joseph Vissarionovich was doing. When Beria told her that Stalin was 'no longer with us', she fainted. Like everyone else accused in this 'affair', Zhemchuzhina was rehabilitated in 1956. But to the end of her days – she died on 1 April 1970 in Moscow at the age of 73 – she remained a fervent, and even fanatical, Stalinist. She also defended the actions of her husband, who had not only divorced her, but actually been encouraged by her to obtain a divorce in light of the accusations levelled against her. Her outward appearance was important to her until the very end. She got a manicure shortly before she died. She was not a 'Party busybody' but rather – to use Nina Berberova's phrase

14 Polina Zhemchuzhina with her husband Vyacheslav
Molotov, Moscow 1963

– an 'iron woman'.[31] At the end of the 1950s, she apparently told Stalin's daughter Svetlana Alliluyeva: 'Your
father was a genius. He destroyed the fifth column in our
country, so when war came the Party and people were
united.'[32] She had nothing but contempt for the post-
Stalin leadership, and she hated Nikita Khrushchev.

The Polina Zhemchuzhina affair was one part of a bigger picture. The global situation had changed radically many times over. Allies in the fight against Hitler drifted apart after the end of the war and the anti-Hitler coalition disintegrated, its camps re-coalescing into the constellation of the Cold War and the division of the world into East and West. It is very plausible that the campaign against Zionism and cosmopolitanism in the late 1940s was conducted with an eye to the nascent Cold War and the conflict around the position of Foreign Minister Molotov. That which had once served the Soviet state – namely, close personal contact with the American ambassador and his wife – subsequently provided material for accusations of conspiracy and espionage. And that which had once spoken in favour of Polina – that she was the second First Lady – spoke against her as soon as the paranoid, ageing Stalin decided his number two man needed to be rebuked and disciplined. Polina Zhemchuzhina's arrest and trial were thus a means of putting pressure on a potential successor to Stalin, who feared for his legacy.[33] Heightened external tensions and the internal threat of a new wave of purges and terror resulted in the rampant obscurantism that characterized the last years of Stalin's dictatorship, which manifested itself in the fight against 'cosmopolitans, agents of American imperialism, and Zionists' and the supposed 'doctors' plot', and which only ended with the dictator's death.[34]

In the moment of threat, however, Stalin found himself facing someone who passionately believed in him, but who defied him by refusing to confess to a single thing, something achieved by very few others in the campaign against cosmopolitans and Zionists – one of them being the biologist Lina Stern, a member of the Academy of Sciences and the Jewish Anti-Fascist Committee, who resisted to the end, a major exception amongst the prisoners tortured and murdered by the secret police.[35] Polina Zhemchuzhina, who was steadfast in interrogations that were tantamount to a show trial, was ultimately saved by Stalin's death on 5 March 1953, but she remained intellectually devoted to him to the end of her days, a more-than-textbook Stalinist.

Her extraordinary career is too wrapped up in the changing times to be dismissed as mere chance. She came from the humble environs of the Jewish shtetl, which she was determined to escape, like many of her peers. She fought underground and joined the Bolshevik Party at a time when it was not clear that it would rise to power. She became something, not thanks to her relationship with Molotov, but mainly because she followed her own path – in her underground activities, her work for women, at the Workers' Faculty and then in the Party cell at the perfume factory, where she soon became the factory director, finally rising to the position of People's Commissar. She was the very embodiment of social advancement through the revolution. She was aware of all that was happening around her during the purges, and she shared the views of her husband, who had personally signed thousands of death warrants and who, even fifty years later in conversation with Felix Chuev, praised Stalin for having eliminated the enemy within, the 'fifth column', before the war, thus guaranteeing victory against the Germans.[36] Her reputation, and apparently her popularity, as the 'Perfume Commissar' were undoubtedly based on two different things: the steely implacability with which she fought her way to the top, and her ability as the manager of the cosmetics trust to give the people something, after a time of chaos and deprivation, that represented a better, more beautiful existence, a touch of luxury in their drab everyday lives. She did nothing less than give the Soviet Union its own unique cosmetics – ones which perhaps could not rival Soir de Paris or Chanel No. 5 for the few who could afford them, but which made life a little bit better for so many others.

Polina Zhemchuzhina got to know the smell of prison (in Lubyanka and Matrosskaya Tishina) and the smell of exile (in Kazakhstan). The first things she demanded after arriving in the steppe city of Kustanai east of the Urals, where the rail line branched off to the newly established Magnitogorsk Metallurgical Combine, were soap, onions and paper. All three items expressed the self-assurance of a woman who would not be beaten down, even after falling from the heights of power into exile at the end of the earth. Soap was the embodiment of basic cleanliness, representing perseverance and discipline in the fight for survival in the camp. Onions represented the fight to maintain physical health and avoid bodily degeneration. And paper represented the fight to preserve one's mental presence and cognitive integrity, if only to write down excerpts from classic Marxist literature and remain intellectually fit enough to absorb the lessons of Stalin's 'Short Course'. The powerful woman who was always austerely and elegantly dressed, the People's Commissar of the Perfume Industry, was plunged into a world that most of her comrades were spared – but one which she was capable of handling, having spent her youth learning the art of survival in the school of the underground.

The fates of the legendary Coco Chanel and largely unknown Polina Zhemchuzhina-Molotova – representatives of worlds of fragrance that were disparate to the point of antagonism, yet also unknowingly connected in many respects – could not be more different. In fact, they are completely asymmetrical. But while each of the women would have considered the other to be the tasteless inhabitant of a totally dissimilar world – one an exemplar of bourgeois decadence, the other a functionary in a despised regime – from the vantage point of the century's end, it is clear that they had much in common.

They both began their lives in the provinces, on the periphery, but they quickly made their way to the political and cultural centres of their respective countries. They wanted to escape their provincial world, but they never cut themselves off from their origins or their families. They always relied on them, returned to them and even maintained relationships when it was extremely risky to do so – such as Zhemchuzhina's connections to her siblings abroad. Both women went with the times, but they did so in their own way. They availed themselves of opportunities, identified the weaknesses in a world dominated by men and drew strength from them in order to grow. They took what high society had to offer, but they were not dependent on it. They came from very different social milieus – petit-bourgeois Catholic on the one hand, petit-bourgeois Jewish on the other – but they wanted to move beyond them. They steered themselves straight into the turbulence of world historical events, which upended everything, but also offered opportunities and career prospects that would have been improbable in the rigid pre-war society. They came from the margins and made their way to the centre. They benefitted from the collapse of order – Zhemchuzhina more so than Chanel; the Russian Revolution seemed to bring an end to discrimination against Jews, clearing the way for unprecedented social and political advancement, and many found themselves catapulted into the highest echelons of power.

They were Nina Berberova's 'iron women': self-reliant, self-confident, energetically working towards their own goals and largely unconcerned with any potential victims they might leave by the wayside. They easily dismissed temporary setbacks, they hit their stride and were mindful of their form. Phenotypically, too, they were close. They resolutely pursued their respective projects: one as a self-made woman, starting with her seamstress shop, her boutiques and her successful

products; the other as an organizer, manager and functionary who was passionately, and even fanatically,
dedicated to 'the cause of the great Stalin' – workaholics
both. One created a world-class private company,
the other led the state trust of a coming superpower.
Chanel occupied a world of wealth, luxury and leisure;
Zhemchuzhina a more ascetic and Spartan milieu. Coco
Chanel had her own houses, villas, her suite at the Ritz,
while Polina Zhemchuzhina lived in the accommodation assigned to her – but at the very centre of the centre
of power, in the Kremlin, the House of Government and
government dachas.

One had a reliably fine instinct and sense of taste, but
no firm convictions otherwise; the other relied on her
skills as well as her beliefs, on her unwavering convic-
tion that everything was as it should be. The Stalin-era
slogan that 'you can't make an omelette without breaking eggs' was also hers. One was shown forbearance
for her disgraceful collaboration and was able to move
abroad to continue living her high-style life, while
the other fell victim to a conspiracy and paid a price
for belonging to the inner circle (as Molotov's wife) –
namely, temporary exclusion from the Communist Party
and demotion to the status of a state pensioner – though
the price was moderate compared to what befell other
victims of the Stalin era. One made no secret of her lifelong dislike for Jews, while the other, though more of a
'non-Jewish Jew' (Isaac Deutscher) on account of being
a communist, ultimately professed to being a 'daughter of the Jewish people' and was punished for it with
charges of 'cosmopolitanism' and 'Zionism'.

And both got off in the end. Chanel was saved by the
end of National Socialism, the liberation of France and
the leniency with which she was punished (or not) for
her collaboration. Zhemchuzhina was freed thanks to
Stalin's death and rehabilitated, but she was unable to
start a second career. Molotov was shunted off to serve

ЖЕМЧУЖИНА—МОЛОТОВА
ПОЛИНА
СЕМЕНОВНА

1 7 — 1970

15   Polina Zhemchuzhina's grave in Moscow

16 Gabrielle Chanel's grave in the Cimetière du
Bois-de-Vaux, Lausanne

as ambassador to the Mongolian People's Republic and
as a delegate to the International Atomic Energy Agency
in Vienna, while Zhemchuzhina studied diligently and
looked after her daughter and grandchild. A romantic
myth soon formed around the elderly couple, that of
a tragic love that lasted until Polina Zhemchuzhina's
death. And, in fact, the many letters that Molotov
sent from New York, Berlin and London to 'Polinka,
my love' ('I have but one desire, to get out of damned
New York and be with you' – 'We'll see each other
soon, I'll kiss and hug you') testify to a fierce love
that lasted for decades.[37] She died on 1 April 1970; he
died at the advanced age of 96 on 8 November 1986.
When Zhemchuzhina was buried in the Novodevichy
Cemetery, the Hymn of the Soviet Union was played, an
honour denied Molotov at his funeral. Perestroika had
begun, and so had the demise of the Soviet Union.[38]

When Coco Chanel returned to the fashion scene,
a new generation of designers was setting the tone,

including Christian Dior and Yves Saint-Laurent. Chanel seemed to be 'out'. But in 1954 she made a comeback. Jean Cocteau celebrated 'Le retour de Mademoiselle Chanel', who resumed her fight against mediocrity and – thanks not least to her income from global sales of Chanel No. 5 – became one of the richest women in France.[39] She died on 10 January 1971 at the age of 87 in her suite at the Ritz. While Molotov and Polina Zhemchuzhina lie buried in the prestigious cemetery of the Novodevichy Convent in Moscow, Chanel was laid to rest outside of France, in the Swiss city of Lausanne.

From another world: the smoke of the crematoria and the smell of Kolyma

It seems almost banal to point out that historical catastrophes have an olfactory side as well. Our knowledge of what took place in the 'Age of Extremes' (Eric Hobsbawm) has been shaped largely by the photographs that captured the unimaginable crimes and atrocities, not by the infernal smells that accompanied them but could not be preserved. And yet, these smells existed. All of the horrific scenes we picture when we think back on the twentieth century are impregnated with odours. We can deduce them from the testimonies of those who perpetrated the horrors and those who survived them. Members of the Nazi death squads on the Eastern Front are reported to have not only imbibed copious amounts of alcohol in order to carry out their crimes, but also to have been supplied with toilet water to help them 'get through the operations'. There are similar reports from the execution squads of the NKVD, which note that, after the executions on the shooting grounds of Butovo and Kommunarka, the officers would remove their rubber aprons and sprinkle themselves with cologne.[1] And in the American films showing Germans being led through the liberated Bergen-Belsen and Buchenwald camps, the Germans can be seen holding handkerchiefs to their noses and turning away from the mountains of skeletal corpses.

If someone were to attempt a follow-up to Alain Corbin's *The Foul and the Fragrant* for the twentieth century, there would be no shortage of material. We have the smell of battlefields enveloped by storms of steel as well as clouds of gas. We have the smell of scorched earth and mass graves, bodies crammed together in deportation trains, pyres of burning books, the smell of the gas piped into the gas chambers and the smoke rising from the crematoria, the stench of decay that only blossoms with the spring thaw when bodies preserved in the frozen ground float free, the burnt smell of cities destroyed by nights of bombing – and, accompanying it all, the smell of deodorized normality in the midst of the crimes, the fragrance of Christmas trees for children during the war, the aromas drifting from celebratory dinners and theatre premieres in the occupied cities.

Hints of what it would take to reconstruct the olfactory landscapes of the twentieth century can be found in endeavours such as Hans J. Rindisbacher's reading of memoirs and witness accounts from German concentration and extermination camps, and in Ekaterina Zhiritskaya's essay on the smells of the Soviet camps.[2]

The totality of sensory perception, including the sense of smell, came into ominous play for a few figures in the early twentieth century. According to the 'Futurist Manifesto' of 1909, written by the bard of Fascism, Filippo Tommaso Marinetti: 'War is beautiful because it unites gunfire, cannonades, ceasefires, and the perfumes and odors of corruption into a symphony . . . Poets and artists of futurism . . . remember these principles of an aesthetics of war so that your struggle for a new poetics and a new sculpture . . . may be enlightened from within!'[3]

Our perception of the world of the camps is also heavily shaped by pictures. This is particularly true of the

German concentration and extermination camps. The names of these factories of death are indelibly associated with images: the gate of Auschwitz-Birkenau through which the trains rolled; the watchtowers and electric fences; the geometrically arranged huts in the blue-prints of I. G. Farben and the aerial photographs of the Allies; the crematoria ovens; the offices and the houses of the guards. But for those who survived the camps or came into contact with them, there is an olfactory dimension to their memories, too: the stench of places where people lived in conditions that would annihilate them, with sanitary facilities and standards of hygiene designed for death. Think of the ghettos, in which tens of thousands of people were crammed together in the smallest of spaces and abandoned to death by starva-tion, exhaustion and epidemics. The olfactory epitome of systematic mass murder is the smell of the smoke billowing from the crematoria, something that crops up again and again in the memories of survivors and people who lived near the camps – but also in the memories of the officials at these death factories. In his autobiog-raphy, Auschwitz commandant Rudolf Hoess writes: 'I had to stand for hours on end in the ghastly stench, while the mass graves were being opened and the bodies dragged out and burned. I had to look through the peep-hole of the gas-chambers and watch the process of death itself, because the doctors wanted me to see it.'

Hoess also says:

It became apparent during the first cremations in the open air that in the long run it would not be possible to continue in that manner. During bad weather or when a strong wind was blowing, the stench of burning flesh was carried for many miles and caused the whole neigh-bourhood to talk about the burning of Jews, despite official counter-propaganda. It is true that all members of the SS detailed for the extermination were bound to

the strictest secrecy over the whole operation, but, as
later SS legal proceedings showed, this was not always
observed. Even the most severe punishment was not able
to stop their love of gossip.[4]

The smell of smoke and ash from the crematoria is
a counterpart to the Nazis' obsessive rhetoric around
cleanliness, purity and hygiene. 'Cleansing of vermin',
'quarantine', 'hygienic measures', 'purity of the blood',
'disinfection' – this is the vocabulary of the systematic
murder carried out along the routes of the advancing
death squads and in the gas chambers. The olfactory
side of Hitler's murderous reign is documented in witness testimony, but it has also been explored in literary
works and memoirs.[5] Holocaust survivor Olga Lengyel
describes the contrast between perfume and smoke as
embodied by the 'blond angel' Irma Grese:

> Where she went she brought the scent of rare perfume.
> Her hair was sprayed with a complete range of tantaliz-
> ing odors: sometimes she blended her own concoctions.
> Her immodest use of perfume was perhaps the supreme
> refinement of her cruelty. The internees who had fallen
> to a state of physical degradation, inhaled these fra-
> grances joyfully. By contrast, when she left us and the
> stale, sickening odor of burnt human flesh, which cov-
> ered the camp like a blanket, crept over us again, the
> atmosphere became even more unbearable.[6]

Primo Levi, a trained chemist, recalls the smell
he perceived when he entered the Buna factory in
Auschwitz-Monowitz: 'How clean and polished the
floor is! . . . The smell makes me start back as if from
the blow of a whip: the weak aromatic smell of organic
chemistry laboratories. For a moment the large semi-
dark room at the university, my fourth year, the mild air
of May in Italy comes back to me with brutal violence
and immediately vanishes.'[7]

In her essay 'The Smell of Kolyma', Ekaterina Zhiritskaya explores the perception of the Soviet camps in the work of Varlam Shalamov, one of the most important Russian writers of the twentieth century. Shalamov spent a total of seventeen years in various camps, but mainly in Kolyma. After he was finally released in 1953, he wrote a collection of stories published as the *Kolyma Tales*. Zhiritskaya suggests that the *Kolyma Tales* should be read with the nose. She points out that Shamalov's awareness revolves primarily around the body, loss of weight, diseases of malnutrition such as pellagra and scurvy, physical degeneration – what was referred to in the Soviet camps as 'alimentary dystrophy'. Shalamov analyses the rapid process of debilitation, systematic exhaustion and dehydration, but also notes the rosy-cheeked, well-fed bodies of other prisoners with their 'excess flesh', something that seems extremely suspicious to the observer. In the camp, the body regains dominance over the mind and mobilizes all of the senses required for survival. This fight for survival sharpens the perception, the 'instinct' and, indeed, the sense of smell:

> The smells of civilisation, culture – all of that belonged to a world that the prisoners of Kolyma had left behind and that no longer mattered. The past life seemed like 'a dream, an invention'. The future did not exist. 'Real were the minute, the hour, the day – from reveille to the end of work. He never guessed further, nor did he have the strength to guess.' You had to survive the present day, and all that mattered was that which helped prolong life and avoid death. And smell in Kolyma – like in the animal kingdom – was a sign of survival or mortal danger.[8]

With its extremely frigid temperatures, Kolyma was free of the smell of death and decay for eight months a year. Snow had a chilly, 'abstract' scent, and in the cold weather, excrement and waste solidified, the latrines froze, the dead became pillars of ice and were stacked like logs in the open air – until spring, when they were uncovered and buried before they could thaw and start to decompose. And the smell of bread stood for survival.

In Auschwitz, the stench of death was always present in the gas and smoke, but the dead in Kolyma, Shalamov writes bitterly, did not smell. 'These "incorruptible dead" were too emaciated, too drained of blood, and were preserved in the permafrost. In the camp, people often died not because they were killed, but because they were not allowed to live.' The characteristic smell in Kolyma, as Zhiritskaya notes, was not the smell of death, but of life:

> Bread topped the prisoner's list of values. In the camp, bread decided everything. To understand what the smell of bread meant in Kolyma, you must reconstruct the context in which it was perceived. In other words, you have to understand what it was for the prisoners. Shalamov's stories provide a whole spectrum of nuances in the perception of bread that are truly fantastic to the average person.

The act of acquiring and eating bread, which is 'commonplace' in normal everyday life, took on a variety of complicated emotional, tactile, gustatory and olfactory nuances in the camp. 'Nothing compares to the feeling of hunger, a gnawing feeling of hunger – the permanent state of the camp inmate, whether he was a 58er [a political prisoner convicted under Article 58] or a *dokhodyaga* [a 'goner'].' Bread was the only source of energy that gave one hope of surviving the next day. Chocolate and condensed milk were nothing but dreams. All that existed in reality, in the here and now, in life as it was – not as an empty fantasy but as an actuality that could be perceived with the senses – was bread. 'Bread turned into the very embodiment of food, the material embodiment of life, into life itself, like the body of Christ in religious rites.' Everything revolved around bread, which determined the course of the day. There was a particular way to consume the bread, to taste it, to hold it in your mouth and chew it. Bread that was left uneaten signalled that the prisoner concerned had given up. And to not receive bread was the equivalent of a death sentence.

The prisoners would do anything to get bread. 'The torture of inaccessible bread is transformed into a torture of smell. This sweet smell of life is one of the most oppressive olfactory dominants in Kolyma. All of the prisoners' human feelings are dulled, but the sense of smell and taste associated with food and aromas are exacerbated to the extreme.' Shalamov writes that a hungry prisoner's 'sensitivity to taste is heightened'. A broth made from frozen greens smells like 'the best Ukrainian borscht', and the aroma of burned kasha 'resembles chocolate'. Shalamov's perception was so radically deformed by his experiences that, even after fifteen years of freedom, potatoes seemed like poison to him.[9]

After the war:
man cannot live on bread alone
– the New Look and *Stilyagi*

After Polina Zhemchuzhina was released and rehabilitated, she did not return to the perfume industry, and
she certainly never held another executive position. But
the industry's reconstruction after the devastation of
the war proceeded without her. More investments were
finally going to be made in light industry, and the needs
of consumers would be taken into account. According
to a decree of the Council of Ministers of the USSR
and the Central Committee of the Communist Party of
the Soviet Union from October 1953, 'Concerning the
Increased Production and Improvement in the Quality
of Food Production', perfume production was to be
doubled. The raw materials came from plantations in
Crimea, Ukraine, Georgia and Central Asia. An All-
Union Scientific Research Institute for Synthetic and
Natural Fragrances (VNIISNDV) had already been
founded in Moscow in 1947. The largest perfume
factory at the time was the Kaluga combine, which
specialized in the production of synthetic odours. It
had been built using the labour of German POWs and
was equipped in part with instruments stemming from

American Lend-Lease shipments during the war. In the mid-1950s, the perfume and cosmetics factories in Leningrad, Kharkov and Mykolaiv, which had been destroyed by the Germans, resumed operations. The factories in Kazan, Sverdlovsk, Tashkent and Tbilisi began to produce civilian goods once again, their range of products was modified, and new brands were introduced, such as Silver Lily-of-the-Valley, Pique Dame and Rusalka. The eau de colognes Shipr and Troynoy were particularly popular in the early 1950s. And, by 1953, the industry had reached its pre-war levels again.[1]

Natalya Dolgopolova, an expert in the history of Soviet perfume, describes the 1950s and 1960s as the 'Golden Age of Soviet perfumery'. The targets in the new Seven-Year Plan (1958 to 1965) were exceeded. A total of around 30,300 tons of perfume, cologne and fragrances were produced in 1965, equating to an average of 130 grams per capita annually, and pushing the USSR past the most important capitalist states in the second half of the 1960s. Fragrances were produced not only for the domestic market, but increasingly also for export; in 1966, more than half a million bottles of perfume were exported to France, Finland, Canada and West Germany, but mainly to Eastern Bloc countries and the Third World.

After the war, the high style of the Stalin era took hold of the perfume industry, and in 1947 a Stalin Prize was awarded for perfume. Perfume bottles were now ornate, and the packaging of the most expensive perfumes resembled artworks made of Atlas silk and polished crystal. These perfumes were meant to reflect the country's increased national pride and patriotism, and they bore names such as Malachite, Amethyst, Sapphire, Native Moscow (for the 800th anniversary of the founding of the capital), and Jubilee of the Soviet Army, packaged in red and gold. The gift sets were of such a high quality that buyers were reluctant to throw them away after the fragrance had been used. In the second half of the 1950s and in the 1960s, the industry moved away from the 'gingerbread style' of the Stalin era to a 'new simplicity' that harked back in many ways to pre-war modernity.

Ilya Ehrenburg's novel *The Thaw* would provide the name for this period.[2] The groundwork for it had been laid right after the war, when the soldiers who had defeated Hitler and got to know Europe in the process returned home hoping that, now that peace had dawned and victory had been achieved, the people would be compensated for their suffering and deprivation, and the rewards of victory would be reaped. While abroad, they had been exposed to a surprisingly high standard of living, even in defeated Nazi Germany. When they returned, they brought not only their experiences and impressions back to the 'fatherland of workers', but also floods of objects from the liberated and occupied territories – everything from furniture, clothing and pianos to feature films and perfumes.

But the people would have to wait. The dictator had to die before the desire for a better life could come to fruition, when hundreds of thousands returned from the camps and it was finally possible to speak of the injustice that had been done and the suffering that had been inflicted. It was a time of opening, when the country's submerged and suppressed potency stirred and came into its own, when improving the present finally seemed to take precedence over creating a utopian future, with homes built for the many instead of gingerbread palaces for the few.

But it was always about more than this, as hinted at by the title of one of Vladimir Dudintsev's most important novels, *Not by Bread Alone*. It was about intellectual freedom, the play of lively creative energies, escape from the confines of decades of patronization, censorship and oppression. Painters discovered the luminous colours and electrifying abstractions of the Soviet avant-garde, which had been scorned under Stalin and disappeared from the public sphere. After years of neoclassical pomp, architects and designers rediscovered the beauty of simple forms and applied their talents to the creation of everyday objects and consumer goods. Counter-culture teens had the confidence to develop their own style and show it off in public, with bright jackets, drainpipe trousers, fedoras. The new realism of Soviet cinema reaped awards in Cannes and Venice; bands played 'Chattanooga Choo Choo' in the Palaces of Culture; scientific disciplines such as sociology and psychology, which had literally been killed off, were re-established; 10,000 young people from every country transformed Moscow into an international city for the World Festival of Youth and Students in 1957; and the Soviet Union had its own young, charismatic hero, Yuri Gagarin, the first man in space. It was a time of optimism and fierce self-confidence in the country's capabilities. Satirical magazines that railed against these 'un-Soviet', 'unpatriotic' and 'decadent' manifestations found themselves futilely swimming against the tide. Red Square was crisscrossed by Dior models, flitting like moths or wondrous creatures from distant stars.[3]

This was the backdrop to the 'Golden Age of Soviet perfumery', which was remarkable for more than just its production numbers and tonnages. The era of the Thaw, too, had its own smell. The range of fragrances expanded, offering something for the most diverse tastes and proclivities, and the scent of the big wide world wafted through the empire that had been closed off for so long. Perfumes reflected important events from the time of the Thaw, and the policy of 'peaceful coexistence' it heralded. They were named after objects of natural beauty – Coral, Crystal, Amber; they quoted works of literature – The Tale of Tsar Saltan, Scheherazade; they referred to mythological figures – Samson, Prometheus,

Bathing Venus, and they increasingly bore names that hinted at intimacy and the private sphere – Violetta, Veronika, Oksana, For You, Only You. The post-Stalin period was dominated by lyrical, romantic names associated with private life: Wedding Perfume, Lirika, Happy Birthday. They additionally reflected the diversity of the multi-ethnic state, with names like My Azerbaijan, Dear Kharkov, Evening Lviv. The diversity of the empire was apparent in the bottles, too; the Tashkent perfume works released creations such as Gur-Emir and Registan, while Tbilisi produced the perfume Iveria, and the factory in Ukraine turned out bottles decorated with traditional Ukrainian folk patterns.

The astonishing variety of fragrances and flacons indicates that the creation of bottles, boxes and gift sets had become a playground for the abundant imagination of Soviet artists and designers. It is therefore all the more unjust, as Dolgopolova rightly points out, that the names of these designers, and around twenty perfumers working in the Soviet Union at the time, were lost to the anonymity of 'work collectives', while the 16,000 members of the Artists' Union were all known by name.[4] In the 1970s, the Soviet perfume industry boasted 700 branded perfume products and 450 branded cosmetics – admittedly still relatively modest compared to the pre-revolutionary production of Rallet & Co. alone, which had 675 brand-name products.[5] An enthusiasm for technology even led to the placement of automats on streets and squares in the early 1960s, where gentlemen could pay 15 kopeks to be spritzed with eau de cologne from 'super-pulverizers'.[6]

But, despite advances in automation, 'chemicalization' and design, the cumbersome planned economy continued to cause problems. Complaints were made about primitively designed labels, poor quality, and deficits on the part of the technical operations responsible for crystal polishing and painting. The industry grappled with the problems typical of a planned economy, including distribution and sales issues, the improper storage of materials resulting in the evaporation of essential oils, and the production of substandard goods due to a lack of work discipline and other factors. Leading perfumer Antonina Vitkovskaya remembers the 'terrible time' under the stifling leadership of Soyuzparfyumerprom and its all-powerful twelve-person 'degustation council'. These twelve 'old dears' were responsible for deciding how the world of fragrances should be composed.[7] But the proposals of experts for reorganizing and streamlining the perfume industry were ignored, reforms were never made, and even socialist competition could not help the situation. As a result, customers turned away and increasingly availed themselves of foreign markets. Queues formed outside cosmetics shops as well. But Soviet women preferred perfumes imported from socialist countries: Chat Noir from Bulgaria, Pani Walewska in blue bottles from Poland, Florena from East Germany. Perfumes were even imported from the Middle East, such as Papillon and Cleopatra from Egypt.

As the country cautiously opened to Western tourists and foreign-exchange transactions began, classic Western perfumes increasingly found their way into the Soviet market as well. Perfumes, like jeans and other Western accessories, were coveted barter items around the hotels for foreigners and in the special shops where tourists, diplomats and Soviet citizens could purchase Western goods for valuta. French perfumes appeared in Moscow in the early 1960s. In the Golden Rose boutique in the Hotel Moskva in the centre of Moscow, it was possible to buy Femme from Rochas and Opium from Yves Saint-Laurent. Long queues formed for Chanel No. 22, which quickly sold out even though it cost 50 roubles, which was exceptionally expensive. Filmmaker Andrei S. Konchalovsky writes of his generation's longing for the fragrances of the wider world: 'I dreamed of Paris back then. It was the city of dreams, the Eiffel Tower, smelling of Chanel and expensive cigarettes.'[8] The 1970s additionally saw the start of partnerships with Western companies, and even joint ventures in the age of Perestroika. Goods labelled 'Paris–Moscow' were easier to sell. A crystal grinding factory named after Mikhail Kalinin, a former Soviet head of state, was renamed Crystal Factory M. Kalinin Moscow–Paris.[9]

One perfume that continued to be popular in the decades after the war was Krasnaya Moskva – though it was slightly modified in 1954, and those familiar with the pre-war fragrance were convinced that the new scent was the same in name only. There have been several generations of the perfume since then, which in the 1970s cost 12 roubles, or a tenth of a worker's average monthly wages, making it one of the more expensive brands. The status of Krasnaya Moskva was confirmed not least by the awards presented to Soviet perfumes at the 1958 Brussels World's Fair, where fragrances such as Krasnaya Moskva and Ogni Moskvi won the gold medal, while Amber from Riga and Northern Light from Leningrad won bronze.[10]

Once again, it was at these expos, the showcases for international achievements, that the world of perfume was reunited. After decades of living in a divided world, it was in Brussels in 1958 that the descendants of Brocard encountered the descendants of Novaya Zarya, the firm that had succeeded Brocard in the Soviet Union. The Thaw and détente had made it possible. And there was more. A certain G. A. Naumenko, a protocol official in the Soviet Foreign Ministry, reported seeking out Coco Chanel in her suite at the Ritz in 1968 and presenting the 85-year-old with a collection of Soviet perfumes: White Lilac and Stone Flower. He said Chanel was genuinely enthused. Roland Barthes writes that Coco Chanel had intended to travel to Moscow to visit a society in need of 'aesthetic innovation', but nothing ever came of this plan. And President Charles de Gaulle's favourite Soviet eau de cologne is said to have been Red Poppy, an Oriental fragrance in a yellow and red box that alluded to the Chinese revolution, apparently created by French perfumer Auguste Michel for the tenth anniversary of the October Revolution.[11]

But Chanel's enthusiasm for the perfumes presented to her and de Gaulle's predilection for Red Poppy did not change the fact that the relationship between the Western and Soviet hemispheres of scent remained asymmetrical, and the age in which Red Moscow held the uncontested hegemony in the world of Soviet perfumes was coming to an end. Other perfumes became popular, Western fragrances made inroads, and celebrities and stars from the Soviet world of beauty and fashion began marketing their own brands. The singer Alla Pugacheva launched a perfume named Alla, and fashion designer Viacheslav Zaitsev released Maroussia – in vintage-style bottles. Even by the end of the 1970s, girls and women were no longer reaching for Red Moscow or Red Poppy, but instead wanted different, fresher, 'greener' fragrances. Krasnaya Moskva, the scent that had, for decades, filled festively illuminated rooms on special occasions – receptions, concerts, art openings – increasingly came to be viewed as an 'old lady's' perfume, indeed the signature fragrance of the Soviet petit bourgeoisie, which the younger generation no longer wanted anything to do with.[12]

And, sometimes, circumstances thought to be long resolved can suddenly catch up with you and blindside you – even thirty years after the end of the Soviet Union, after the grey of the Soviet world has been washed away and long forgotten and Moscow has become a nexus of luxury and fashion, in a place not far from GUM on Nikolskaya Street – known as the 25th of October Street in Soviet times, connecting Lubyanka Square and Red Square. This is a glittering shopping street, just as it was before the revolution, now lined with the outposts of international fashion labels.

For years, the façade of 23/1–2 Nikolskaya Street has been shrouded by giant tarpaulins advertising menswear from the Billionaire label. As of 2020, there are plans to turn the building into a retail centre to give the new Moscow elite, who have already seen Milan, Paris and London, precisely what they are looking for: fashion, expensive accessories, a bookshop, a wine merchant, restaurants – and a perfume boutique. The building has a history. The eclectic façade comes from the 'Gründerzeit' period of the nineteenth century, but between 1935 and the end of the 1940s the building housed the Military Collegium of the Supreme Court of the USSR and was a key site in the Great Terror of the Stalin era. And it is here that the building's current owner, Vladimir Davidi – said to be a sensitive spirit who appreciates art, knows the madeleine passage from Proust and cannot imagine a life without Mozart or Monet – wants to open a boutique for his company Esterk Lux Parfum.

The building served as the headquarters of the Moscow Military District from the 1950s, but after the end of the Soviet Union it stood empty for a while and changed hands several times. In the Moscow of Mayor Yury Luzhkov, historical buildings were demolished left and right to make way for underground parking garages and offices; only the façades were to remain. But there was resistance, because 23 Nikolskaya Street is not just any building. Tens of thousands of people were sentenced to death here in 1937. Underground tunnels connected it to other NKVD buildings on Lubyanka Square. At a desk on the ground floor, the family members of detainees would queue up to find out what had happened to their relatives. The first floor held the office of Vasiliy Ulrikh, Chairman of the Military Collegium of the Supreme Court of the USSR and the judge who presided over many Moscow show trials. On the second floor was the courtroom where the Military Collegium pronounced 31,456 death sentences between October 1936 and the end of November 1938 – 7,408 for the city of Moscow alone – and sentenced 6,857 people to incarceration in prisons and camps. The court proceedings usually lasted no longer than twenty minutes. The court convicted and executed 25 People's Commissars of the Soviet Union, 19 People's Commissars of the Union Republics, and thousands of Army commanders, intellectuals and combine directors. The people convicted and executed here included Marshals of the Soviet Union Mikhail Tukhachevsky and Alexander Yegorov, members of the 'Bolshevik Guard', the parents of ballerina Maya Plisetskaya, the director Vsevolod Meyerhold, and writers such as Isaac Babel and Boris Pilnyak. Many of them were horrifically tortured before being shot and burned in the crematorium of Donskoye Cemetery.

And this building is now supposed to house a perfume boutique. It is thanks solely to the organization known as Memorial that the building was not torn down, and that the fight to transform this monstrous crime scene into a place of mourning and remembrance continues. In October 2019, tens of thousands of people signed a petition by *Novaya Gazeta* newspaper calling for a museum of political repression to be established at the site. Alexei Nesterenko, a man now in his eighties, whose father was shot in the building in 1937, has protested outside 23 Nikolskaya Street for years to draw attention to the importance of the place. Activists point out that traces of the past are still visible here: the wrought-iron stairs and banisters, the oak flooring in Ulrikh's office, a cartridge box discovered in 2007 in the basement, where a kitchen and wine merchant are now supposed to be built. An article in *Novaya Gazeta* proposed that the names of the executed should be projected onto the building's façade at night. It even suggested naming a perfume *Pulya v zatylok* – 'Bullet in the back of the head' – as a protest against turning a site of murder into a temple of consumption.

And, in fact, a fragrance has been composed in protest, with a name that plays on the number of Chanel's perfume and the address of the building on Nikolskaya Street: 'Composition No. 23 opens with notes of the old papers and inks that were used to sign the death sentences. The story continues with the aroma of a damp basement, soon followed by the main ingredient: the sharp smell of gunpowder, which is gradually replaced by a note of ash, leaving behind a bitter aftertaste.'[13]

Excursus:
the *grande dame* of German film Olga Chekhova, cosmetics and the dream of eternal youth

Even during her lifetime, Olga Chekhova was known as the '*grande dame* of German film'. When she died in 1980 at the age of 83 in Munich, she had a glittering career behind her. She worked on around 140 films, usually in leading roles, occasionally as the director. Her filmography reveals that she was sometimes involved in multiple productions in a single year. She appeared alongside the most famous actors and worked with the most important directors (Max Ophüls, Carl Froelich, Wolfgang Liebeneiner). Her films cover an incredibly broad repertoire of themes, including Russia (*Burning Border, Double-Agent Asew*), literary works (*Nora, Debit and Credit, Peer Gynt, Bel Ami*) and Prussia (*The Mill at Sanssouci, The Hymn of Leuthen, Trenck, Andreas Schlüter*). But the vast majority were comedies, love stories and melodramas (*The Three from the Filling Station, Artists Love, Masquerade in Vienna, Waltz around the Stefanstower* and many others). Her first film was with Friedrich Murnau in 1921, and she was one of the few to successfully make the leap from the age of silent film to talkies.

She began acting in Russia, but in the Weimar era she became one of the defining stars of the UFA film company.[1] She reached the peak of her popularity in the Nazi period and continued her film career after the war, with astonishing continuity and new takes on old themes and roles under different directors (*Maharadscha wider Willen, Das Geheimnis einer Ehe, Everything for Father*). For an entire generation, she was the embodiment of the elegant yet capable and vivacious woman. While many fellow actors and directors she had worked with either chose, or were forced, to leave Germany and go into exile after 1933, she not only stayed but became part of the society that Nazi bigwigs liked to surround themselves with at their receptions when they wanted to appear cosmopolitan and civil. This particularly applied to Joseph Goebbels, Joachim von Ribbentrop and her greatest admirer, Adolf Hitler, with whom she was photographed, in all of her beauty, while seated next to him at a summer party.

This career was quite astounding for a woman from the 'Chekhov clan' (Renata Helker). Her aunt was Olga Knipper-Chekhova, Anton Chekhov's wife and a legendary actor with the Moscow Art Theatre; her husband was the actor Michael Chekhov, who had a career in Hollywood after he emigrated; and her daughter, Olga, and granddaughter, Vera, carried on the tradition of this important family of artists and actors in the Federal Republic of Germany.[2] But her life story is emblematic of the twentieth century, with her origins in a German-Russian family in Moscow, escape from the Russian Civil War, the enticement of Weimar culture, the fatal juxtaposition and interplay of cinematic illusion and Nazi barbarism, and a new beginning that was hardly new at all in post-war West Germany.

The extent to which she was caught up in the tides of the times became apparent in discussions triggered by reports of her actual or suspected work for the Soviet secret service. We know that Olga Chekhova was arrested in her house in the Gatow district of Berlin at the end of April 1945, after the Red Army had arrived. She was flown to Moscow and interrogated for three months by officials from the counter-intelligence organization SMERSh and the NKVD before being brought back to Berlin in August. The files that have come to light do not prove that she was an agent for the Soviet intelligence service, but they do reveal that she was squeezed and exploited as a source – not least by her brother, the composer Lev Knipper, who also worked for the secret service.[3]

Olga Chekhova's life is relevant to the history of the scents of the empire, but not on account of her achievements as an actor, her association with the leadership of the 'Third Reich' or any speculation about her connection to Soviet intelligence. Olga Chekhova not only had 'three lives' – in Russia, in pre-war and Nazi Germany, and in West Germany – she also had two careers, two professions: she was a trained, and indeed certified, cosmetician. As she writes in her not entirely reliable – and often actually misleading – memoirs, at the end of her film career she started a second life: 'I sell my house in Kladow and move from Berlin to Munich. Right in the centre of the Bavarian metropolis, I open my first cosmetics salon.'[4] Banking on her fame as a film star, she founded the company Olga Tschechowa Kosmetik OHG in 1955, which initially had 7, and later 100, employees. She set up a laboratory, hired chemists and developed her own formulations. She was extremely committed to the company, selling her jewellery and pawning her antiques to fund it. Above all, she worked professionally:

Cosmetic knowledge acquired decades earlier, at home and abroad, and continually expanded: a degree from Brussels, a degree from the 'Université de Beauté' in Paris, lectures attended at the universities in Berlin and Munich, in-depth conversations and consultations with the famous Russian biologist Professor Dr Bogomolets in London, who additionally encouraged me to create my own formulas. I take from this the insight that it is possible to promote the regeneration of the body and its cells – but not solely through the application of various organic substances. The patient must consistently and actively contribute – with a largely toxin-free diet, for example.[5]

Chekhova established her own perfume-production operation, as evidenced by the list of perfumes she created: Annonce, Chapitre, Madame, Mademoiselle, Monsieur Tschechowa, Nancy, Theoreme, Vesna, Dushenka and Green Season, all produced by the cosmetics firm in Munich.[6]

But what was more important was her reputation – and the marketing of her reputation – as an 'ageless woman', a beauty and cosmetics consultant, a lecturer and an advisor. The books she wrote or co-edited after the war and during the 'economic miracle' years are titled accordingly: *Chatting about Beauty*, with illustrations by the author herself; and *Ageless Woman: A Beauty and Fashion Guide*, which can be read as a manual for people working in the cosmetics industry, with expert 'cosmetological' input from doctors, biologists and chemists.[7] Veering between a conversational tone and encyclopaedic detail, the latter book addresses central issues in beauty care: its medical basis as well as formulas for fighting wrinkles, the functionality of hormones and sebaceous glands as well as tips for getting a good night's sleep and eating well, and pointers on facial treatments and the 'Mecca of fragrances'. The

17 Olga Chekhova

leading perfumes, in Chekhova's opinion, are recited in
a kind of perfumology: Chanel No. 5, Lelong, Lanvin,
Schiaparelli, Dior, Patou.[8]

Her main message, however, is not so much technical

or hygienic, but has to do instead with the attitude she says people should develop if they want to stay youthful. Chekhova writes that she was always being asked to 'reveal the secret of her perpetual youth and freshness'. She says she believes not in miracle cures but in self-discipline, in the importance of a certain lifestyle:

> a positive attitude towards the vicissitudes of life with all of its joys, cares, hardships and disappointments; the attitude and approach towards one's fellow human beings, the choice of friends, the way of dealing with friends and strangers, the tidiness of the home, the attitude towards family, the treatment of animals and indeed all living creatures, in short: proving oneself in the course of each day with all of its joys and woes!

This boils down to the maxims found in self-help books: 'Take absolutely everything as it comes.' 'Don't take yourself too seriously.' 'Try to create your paradise here on earth. (There might not be one otherwise!) Dwell within it as someone who loves beauty.'[9]

There is a good deal of evidence that Chekhova's philosophy of a beautiful and successful life was more than just a rhetorical figure. In her memoirs, she mentions the degree she earned at the 'Université de Beauté' in Paris and her conversations with a certain 'Dr Bogomolets'. Her 'Université de Beauté' may well be the Académie Scientifique de Beauté, which was founded in 1890 and has been 'at the service of beauty' ever since. The academy opened the ur-version of a professional beauty salon at 376 rue Saint Honoré in Paris, released the first *Manual for Women's Beauty Needs*, opened the first cosmetics school and published science-based cosmetics guides. It won a gold medal at the Exposition Coloniale Internationale in Paris in 1931, and received the first cosmetics patent in 1936. For the 125th anniversary of its founding in 2015, the academy recounted its history on its website: 'The company has been putting its expertise at the service of beauty for more than a century. From the famous "Princesse des Crèmes" or "Princesse des Poudres" without forgetting the "Rubis Pompadour", the Maison has been astonishing the whole world since it was created.'[10]

But who is the 'Dr Bogomolets' mentioned in Chekhova's memoirs? It can only be Alexander Alexandrovich Bogomolets (1884–1946), a physician born in Ukraine to an intelligentsia family with subversive tendencies, who published pioneering works in the fields of pathophysiology, immunology and gerontology. He was the driving force behind the establishment of the Ukrainian Academy of Sciences and received multiple scientific awards, including the Stalin Prize in 1941, Hero of Socialist Labour in 1944, two Orders of Lenin, the Order of the Patriotic War, and the Order of the Red Banner of Labour.[11] In 1937, he was elected as a deputy of the Supreme Soviet, and was probably the most prominent representative of Soviet science to visit the international exposition in Paris, where Olga

18 Alexander A. Bogomolets

Knipper-Chekhova had performed with the Moscow Art Theatre.

Bogomolets had enjoyed an impressive career by that point. He became a professor at a young age and was admired by the physiologist and Nobel Prize-winner Ivan P. Pavlov. He visited the Sorbonne before World War I and actively supported women's rights. While working in Saratov during the Russian Civil War, he set up an epidemiological laboratory using his own funds and developed a serum – the 'Bogolomets serum' – which was designed to stimulate the immune system to heal wounds and fractures, and which would play a major role in treating wounded soldiers during World War II. He also developed methods for blood transfusion and preservation, founded the *Physiological Journal*, and helped to build up the Ukrainian Academy of Sciences in Kiev, becoming its president in 1930.

His creation of an Institute of Gerontology, and the book he published in 1939, *The Prolongation of Life*, point to one of his main scientific interests: the fight against premature ageing. He was convinced that it would be possible to extend human life to 150 years

19 Edition of the book by Alexander A. Bogomolets,
The Prolongation of Life, Kiev, 1939

in the future. The Institute for Blood Transfusion founded by 'Lenin's rival' Alexander Bogdanov – where Bogomolets also worked – indicates that the notion that illness – and even death – could potentially be defeated was very much in the air during the Soviet awakening of the 1920s.[12] Statements by Trotsky and prominent representatives of the biocosmism movement are evidence of this. The search for ways to prolong life that occupied Alexander Bogomolets – and that also interested Stalin, whose dictatorship ended the lives of millions – was eminently compatible with Olga Chekhova's dream of the 'ageless woman', a dream that knew no borders.

How One World smells

For many people, the dissolution of the Soviet Union was not, as President Putin claimed in 2005, the 'greatest geopolitical disaster of the twentieth century'. It was, instead, a series of small – and sometimes even fortunate – disasters, including in the Soviet cosmetics and perfume industry. Influential centres of perfume production were suddenly located 'abroad', in different states. Dzintars in Riga, Alye Parusa in Kiev, Iveria in Tbilisi and others found themselves in newly independent republics, their supplies of essential oils from plantations in Crimea and Central Asia interrupted, their sales networks shut down. Above all, the prestige of domestic brands – even those that had been established over generations – was gone, unable to withstand the pressure of the foreign brands crowding into the Russian market.[1] The logos of global companies appeared in the centres of big Soviet cities: Rochas, Guerlain, Dior, Cartier, Gucci and all the others. Flagship stores now opened not just in New York, Tokyo, Hong Kong or Shanghai, but also on Tverskaya Street and in Luxury City in Moscow. Major domestic cosmetics and perfume companies such as Novaya Zarya / New Dawn and Severnoye Siyaniye / Northern Light were taken over and placed under foreign management or shut down altogether, either temporarily or permanently.

And highly specialized noses detected something else. It was not just the names of the cosmetics firms that had disappeared, but also the specific smell of Soviet perfumes. New essences from new parts of the world had given rise to different fragrances with different notes and aromas. Concerned connoisseurs of Soviet and Russian perfume wondered whether these new scents, as seductive as they were, could still be considered scents of the Russian fatherland. They bemoaned the decline in quality previously assured by strict production-control standards, and they complained about the masses of counterfeit perfumes flooding the country. After the socialist distribution system collapsed, hundreds of thousands of 'shopping tourists' had set about supplying the country with necessities while creating added value for themselves to keep their families afloat in times of crisis. Hundreds of thousands of these shopping tourists and petty traders shuttled back and forth, week after week, month after month, to maintain trade links within the country and between Russia and the world outside. Hundreds of thousands of people commuted between Moscow and Dubai, Odessa and Istanbul, Leningrad / Saint Petersburg and Helsinki, Sverdlovsk/ Yekaterinburg and Tianjin to sustain the circulation of goods, without which the country's supply system probably would have collapsed. They dealt in food and consumer goods of all sorts.

In the 1990s, anyone roaming the bazaars outside the Olympic Stadium in Moscow, at the terminal stations of the Metro in Saint Petersburg, or the biggest market in south-eastern Ukraine, the Seventh-Kilometre near Odessa, would find huge trading centres that had sprung up overnight, proper caravanserais with everything they entail: cross-country bus stations, police stations, fast-food restaurants, night shelters, veritable cities made of tents and shipping containers stacked on top of one another, recalling the original centres of trade – souks,

medieval market halls, teeming fairgrounds, the world
of arcades. 'Black market' does not really describe this
phenomenon, as everything took place in the open,
on expanses covering many square kilometres at the
edge of the city. For a long moment, this informal but
real economy overran the formal economy, which was
statistically accounted for but fictional. There was nothing you could not find there: Reebok, Adidas, Turkish
leather goods, Italian fashion labels, Korean consumer
electronics, apple juice from Germany, condoms, wedding dresses, bathroom fittings, an endless list, a true
representation of the needs of a society that had fallen
out of step. And fragrances, of course, from every
brand in the world, in every price range, purchased in
Istanbul, Naples, Alexandria, Urumqi and resold in the
farthest corners of the Russian provinces. Every make
was available, from Armani, through Cartier, Chanel
and Elizabeth Arden, to Ermenegildo Zegna – all counterfeit, naturally. At the time, it was not the authenticity
of the product but rather the name and the label that
gave the wearer the status of success. The new emerging
markets of the Eastern Bloc were, in reality, fragmented
parallel markets, with zones of luxury consumption
marked out by flagship stores and sumptuous boutiques
on the one hand, and bazaars with knock-off brands
that regular people could afford on the other.[2]

The momentum with which international cosmetic
and perfume corporations descended upon the new
markets of the former Eastern Bloc, and the speed with
which they established themselves in prime locations
in post-Soviet cities, said something not only about the
weakness of Soviet brands, but also about the clout of
the luxury companies that had joined the ranks of the
most powerful global players in the second phase of
globalization.[3] Vuitton, Elizabeth Arden, Prada, Chanel
– they all appeared on the scene overnight. The biggest
international luxury firms presented their collections

in prestigious locations; Karl Lagerfeld opted for the Maly Theatre in Moscow.[4] Western fashion houses played with the great heritage of Russia, the luxury of the Russian aristocracy, the refinement of the Silver Age and the electrifying forms of the Russian avant-garde. Vuitton celebrated its company jubilee with a two-storey-high Vuitton suitcase showcasing the company's history, erected on Red Square in front of the brightly lit façade of GUM department store and within view of the Lenin mausoleum.[5] The triumphal march of Western perfumes was just one (albeit fundamental) feature of a lifestyle revolution in the city centres of the former Soviet Union. This 'scenery change' – the cryptic euphemism for revolution in nineteenth-century Russian literature – took place on every level. People refurnished their houses, travelled to the Canary Islands and Venice, switched to French cheese and red wine.

The reaction against what some viewed as a foreign invasion was not long in coming. Many set off on a search for the lost time that had taken the scents of the Soviet epoch with it. Old brands were remade and enjoyed new popularity. Krasnaya Moskva was available again. A new-old pride emerged, as did new efforts to hunt down traces and relics of the lost world. Almost every bazaar and flea market had at least one table of perfume bottles from the Soviet or pre-revolutionary era, watched over by specialists with intimate knowledge of the material and sought out by connoisseurs passionately dedicated to expanding their private collections. The internet is full of portals for posting discoveries, losses, erudite commentary, photos from family albums. In the virtual world, the perfume bottle has become a fulcrum around which the collective memory of an entire generation revolves. Museums for perfume and cosmetics have opened as well, such as the Moscow Museum of Fashion at 4 Ilyinka Street in Kitay-Gorod, and the Moscow Perfume Museum at 36/2 Arbatskaya

Ulitsa. Opulent coffee-table books have been published, recounting the history of Russian perfume through the bottles themselves. And, inevitably, the prices of vintage bottles have skyrocketed. A few years ago, a bottle of Troynoy cologne – unopened – would set you back 35,000 roubles, or about 700 euros. Such treasures can still be found, just as soon as you pass through the duty-free perfume zone in the airport and leave its generic smell behind you.

Not only the *Black Square*: Malevich's perfume bottle

In this tide of memory, nostalgia and the search for a beauty regarded as lost, a place must be reserved for the discovery of Kazimir Malevich's perfume bottle. In late 2017, an exhibition opened in Moscow at the 'Worker and Kolkhoz Woman' pavilion, a building topped by Vera Mukhina's monumental sculpture which once crowned the Soviet pavilion at the Paris expo in 1937. The telling title of the exhibition was 'Not only the *Black Square*'. Even an audience long familiar with Malevich was surprised by the show's sensational revelation that Malevich had designed the bottle for one of the most popular Soviet fragrances: Severny eau de cologne. Kazimir Malevich, whose *Black Square* had kicked open the door to abstraction in modern art, was suddenly revealed to be the designer of an object as mundane as a perfume bottle – before the revolution, no less!

Alexandra Shatskikh, probably the world's foremost expert in Malevich and Chagall, had been following this trail for some time, and now it was confirmed. Shatskikh is closely acquainted with Malevich's descendants and had found hints in their house that in Malevich's early years – right after he returned from Kursk to Moscow and had to support his family – he relied in part on commercial jobs that seemed to have little or nothing to do with his calling as an artist. He made posters, advertisements, illustrations – and he designed objects. Alexander Brocard, who had taken over his father's company, was an art enthusiast and collector who hired Malevich to draft a design for Severny ('North') cologne.[1] This must have been in the early 1910s, according to Alexandra Shatskikh. Malevich had already distinguished himself with his Impressionist–Symbolist paintings, luminous landscapes and portraits. He took the design job simply to earn a living. But in just a few years (around 1915 or 1916), he would paint *Black Square*, thus delivering the statement that would make him world famous as a pioneer of abstraction and founder of Suprematism.[2]

Malevich devised a three-part bottle with a total height of about 19.5 centimetres. The frosted crystal was laced with a fine web of crackle (*craquelé*) and sealed with a glass stopper. The stopper was encased in an irregular knob of glass clearly meant to be an iceberg, and perched on its peak was a meticulously sculpted polar bear, clinging to the glass as if trying not to slide off. Its paws, coat, tail and face were soft and exquisitely cut. Malevich's design was technically implemented by the artist Adel Yakovlevna Yakobson, who specialized in glasswork, which is probably one of the reasons the name of the design's originator was forgotten. The bear on top of the iceberg became the trademark of Severny cologne from the day the bottle was launched in 1911 until its production was provisionally discontinued in 1996. Millions upon millions of bottles were sold, making Severny the most popular cologne in the Soviet Union, alongside Shipr and Troynoy. Generations would remember the bottle, and millions grew up with the polar bear, which was eventually slightly modified and lost some of its detail, but was still easily identifiable as the brand's trademark. A true emblem, a true *lieu de mémoire*.[3]

Malevich must have had to familiarize himself with

20 Kazimir Malevich's bottle for Severny ('North') eau
de cologne with polar bear, 'Flakon Malevicha'

the details of bottle manufacturing, such as how the
glass was ground. Some of his pictures hint at this,
including the Cubist paintings *Knife Grinder* and *Vanity
Case.*[4] Based on an advertising poster for Severny showing a polar bear against a dark backdrop with a rising
sun, Alexandra Shatskikh convincingly argues that there
is also a direct line from this sunlit background to the
opera *Victory over the Sun,* which Malevich worked on
with other avant-gardists such as Velimir Khlebnikov,
Mikhail Matyushin and Aleksei Kruchenykh. The opera
premiered in 1913 and was taken as the founding
manifesto of a revolutionary Futurist *Gesamtkunstwerk*
– almost a temporal parallel, one might say, to what
Malevich's compatriot and contemporary Sergei
Diaghilev had created with the Ballets Russes in Paris.[5]
    Malevich's perfume bottle with the polar bear also
reflects something of the spirit of the times. At the
start of the twentieth century, the scramble for the
North Pole, the last remaining *terra incognita*, was in

21 Bottle of Rallet No. 1

full swing. Frederick Cook set out for the North Pole in 1908, and Robert Peary followed a year later, in a race that captivated the whole world. After the Russian Revolution, conquering and claiming the north had become a state programme for the Soviet power. Flights over the North Pole and the opening of the Northeast Passage were major mass media and propaganda events in the 1930s.[6] The eau de cologne named 'North', which was embodied by a polar bear, thus became a permanent fixture in everyday Soviet life.

Perhaps this revelation will re-ignite the discussion of the origins of the Chanel No. 5 bottle. It may be that the Spartan, minimalist glass cube now honoured in the Museum of Modern Art in New York has less to do with the minimalism and geometric abstraction of someone like Piet Mondrian, as art historians sometimes

22 *Shtof* bottles

assume, and is more likely to have been based on the
simple shape of the drinking vessel customarily carried
by tsarist officers and referred to by the Germanic-Baltic
name *shtof* – since there is a good deal of evidence that
this vodka flask was the model for the bottle of the perfume that Ernest Beaux had presented as Rallet No. 1
back in 1914, several years before Chanel No. 5.[7]

As for the Severny cologne bottle, millions of people,
for generations and decades, used an everyday product
that had been designed by the genius Kazimir Malevich
– and they never knew it. By merging sophisticated
design with the utility of a mass-produced object, the
bottle was the realization of the avant-garde dream
of aesthetically shaping everyday life, but without the
creator or consumer realizing it. Over the course of
a century, through all of the caesuras, upheavals and

catastrophes, art and the everyday world had found a way to unite – practically behind the backs of producers and consumers alike.

Now that the 'Age of Extremes' has come to an end, it is time to pull together the stories that ran parallel, and often counter, to one another for so long, despite their common origin. We must look back to the first age of globalization, the one blasted apart by World War I and the Russian Revolution, when ingenious perfumers took a single drop of fragrance and produced two lines, each of which became the epitome of scent and the seductive power of beauty for millions. These two developments had more in common than anyone realized at the time.

Now that these underground, unconscious connections have been laid bare, they can be displayed together and next to each other. A world archive and museum of fragrances would be the right setting for this – perhaps in Grasse on the Riviera, where everything began and there is already a museum; or in the Osmothèque in Versailles, so close to Paris, the capital of perfume; or in Moscow, a city in the process of assuring itself of its own history – or, indeed, in the Museum of Modern Art in New York, where Krasnaya Moskva, and even Kazimir Malevich's polar bear on an iceberg, could take their place alongside Chanel No. 5.

Notes

* I first picked up the trail leading to Chanel No. 5 and Red Moscow when writing my book *Das sowjetische Jahrhundert* ('The Soviet Century').

The scent of the empire

1 Here and throughout the book, I am following the biography of Gabrielle Chanel written by Edmonde Charles-Roux, *Chanel and Her World*, first published in French in 1979. There are many other accounts of her life; see, e.g., Axel Madsen, *Coco Chanel*; Paul Morand, *The Allure of Chanel*. Regarding Grasse as the 'Rome of fragrances', see *Grasse*.
2 Tilar J. Mazzeo, *The Secret of Chanel No. 5*, pp. 60ff.
3 Ibid., p. 61; Marie-Dominique Lelièvre (*Le No 5 de Chanel*, p. 43) speaks of a 'grey zone' regarding the date and location of the meeting.
4 Quoted in Konstantin M. Verigin, *Blagoukhannost'*, p. 50 (in the online edition at www.e-reading. club/book.php? book=1016413). French edition: Constantin Weriguine, *Souvenirs et parfums*.
5 Mazzeo, *The Secret of Chanel No. 5*, pp. 62, 67;

regarding the formula for Chanel No. 5, see https:// en.wikipedia.org/wiki/Chanel_No._5.

6 Mazzeo, *The Secret of Chanel No. 5*, p. 65.

7 Ibid., pp. 65f.

8 For various accounts of the perfume's creation, see Michael Edwards, *Perfume Legends*, p. 43, and Joachim Laukenmann, 'Es riecht nach Remake'. Regarding the different versions of the story, see, e.g., https://de.wikipedia.org/wiki/Chanel_No_5. The most important analysis of the genealogy of Chanel No. 5 can be found in Philip Kraft et al., *From Rallet No 1 to Chanel No 5 versus Mademoiselle Chanel No 1*. However, like most accounts, this article disregards the line leading from Brocard's Bouquet de Catherine to Krasnaya Moskva.

9 This formula can be found at https://de.wikipedia. org/wiki/Chanel_ No_5.

10 Mazzeo, *The Secret of Chanel No. 5*, p. 71.

11 Karl Lagerfeld, *Chanel's Russian Connection*.

12 Mazzeo, *The Secret of Chanel No. 5*, p. 72.

13 Ibid., pp. 72, 67f.

14 Jean-Louis Froment, *No. 5 Culture Chanel*, introduction.

15 *Zolotoy yubiley parfyumernogo proizvodstva Tovarishchestva Brokar i Ko v Moskve*.

16 Regarding the nationalization of factories after 1917, see Manfred Hildermeier, *Geschichte der Sowjetunion*, pp. 105–56.

17 Regarding food procurement, foraging trips and the black market, see Aleksandr Y. Davydov, *Meshochniki i diktatura v Rossii 1917–1921*.

18 Natalya Dolgopolova, *Parfyumeriya v SSSR*, I, pp. 57ff.

19 Ibid., p. 124. The perfume is said to recall the scent of a bouquet, with notes that gradually emerge on the skin; see https://fanfact.ru/duhi-krasnaja-moskva-pridumal-francuzskij-parfjumer.

20 This is according to Marina Koleva, 'Sovetskaya parfyumeriya', pp. 74–85 (here p. 80); Viktoriya Wlasowa, 'Krasnaya Moskva'; Nina Nazarova, '"Krasnaya Moskva"'.

21 Dolgopolova, *Parfyumeriya v SSSR*, I, p. 125; 'Medvedevu podarili dukhi pochti stoletney vyderzhki', RIA Novosti, 10 October 2011, https://ria.ru/20111010/454649754.html.

22 An article by an R. Kronhaus in the magazine *Technika Molodezhi* (p. 27) says that he first arrived in 1908; Koleva, 'Sovetskaya parfyumeriya', p. 80; Dolgopolova, *Parfyumeriya v SSSR*, I, p. 125.

23 Hopefully the documents in the Novaya Zarya company archives will clarify the identity of the two perfumes once and for all.

24 Other authors seem to have no doubt that Krasnaya Moskva was derived directly from The Empress's Favourite Bouquet; see Dolgopolova, *Parfyumeriya v SSSR*, I, p. 126. The continuity between the two perfumes has been confirmed by Isabelle Chazot of the Osmothèque in Versailles (10 July 2020). Despite being in competition, the relationship between Rallet and Brocard was extremely close. For example, Rallet produced perfume bottles for Brocard (according to Nicolas Maunoury of La Glass Vallée, Pôle Mondial du flaconnage de luxe de la Vallée de La Bresle, 28 September 2020).

25 Dolgopolova, *Parfyumeriya v SSSR*, I, p. 130.

26 Dolgopolova, *Parfyumeriya v SSSR*, I, pp. 66, 67ff.

27 Regarding TeZhe, see Veniamin Kozharinov, *Russian Perfumery*, pp. 122, 123; also see Jukka Gronow, *Caviar with Champagne*.

Scentscapes

1 Somewhat different dates for the production and presentation of the perfume (1925/1927) are found in Schlögel, *Das sowjetische Jahrhundert*, pp. 250–63.

2 Regarding the Chanel No 5. exhibit at the Museum of Modern Art, see *The Package*, Museum of Modern Art Bulletin, vol. 27, no. 1, Fall 1959, available online at https://assets.moma.org/documents/moma_catalogue_1953_300190180.pdf.

3 Arthur Gold and Robert Fizdale, *Misia*, p. 215.

4 Some attribute the phrase to the Finns, who used it to refer to their weapons in the Soviet–Finnish Winter War; others trace it back to a decree issued by Molotov.

5 Even the exhibition in the Palais de Tokyo takes a Western-centric view of the history of Chanel's perfume, aside from references to Diaghilev and Stravinski, etc.

6 Constance Classen et al., *Aroma*; regarding the sociology of smell, see Jürgen Raab, *Soziologie des Geruchs*.

7 Quoted in Alain Corbin, *The Foul and the Fragrant*, p. v.

8 Jonathan Reinarz, *Past Scents*, pp. 209, 216, 217, 218. Russian research has been collected in volumes edited by Olga Vainshtein, *Aromaty i zapakhi v kul'ture*; Olga Vainshtein, *Dendi*; Irina A. Mankevich, *Povsednevnyy Pushkin*; Olga Kushlina, 'Ot slova k zapakhu', pp. 102–10; Maria Pirogovskaya, *Miazmy, simptomy, uliki*.

9 Georg Friedrich Wilhelm Hegel, *Phenomenology of Spirit*, p. 331.

10 Immanuel Kant, *Anthropology from a Pragmatic Point of View*, pp. 50f.

11 Friedrich Nietzsche, *Ecce homo*, p. 88.
12 Friedrich Nietzsche, *Thus Spoke Zarathustra*, p. 408.
13 Konstantin M. Verigin, *Blagoukhannost'*, and Arthur Schopenhauer, *The World as Will and Representation*, p. 31.
14 George Orwell, *The Road to Wigan Pier*, quoted in Classen et al., *Aroma*, p. 166.
15 Somerset Maugham, quoted in Classen et al., *Aroma*, p. 166.
16 Marcel Proust, *In Search of Lost Time*, vol. I: *Swann's Way*, pp. 60–5.

When 'the weakest link breaks in the imperialist chain' (Lenin)

1 Viktor Lobkovich, *Zolotoy vek russkoy parfyumerii i kosmetiki 1821–1921*.
2 See Vladimir Ilyich Lenin's classic work *The Development of Capitalism in Russia* from 1899, and Leo Trotzky's *Results and Prospects* from 1906.
3 The works by Viktor Lobkovich, Veniamin Kozharinov and Natalya Dolgopolova, and (above all) the discourse on the internet, are representative of the intense interest in this subject.
4 See *Russland 1900* ('Russia 1900'), ed. Ralf Beil, catalogue of the exhibition held at the Mathildenhöhe Darmstadt Institute in 2008.
5 Regarding cloister gardens, see Dmitriy S. Likhachev, *Poeziya sadov*.
6 Lobkovich, *Zolotoy vek russkoy parfyumerii i kosmetiki 1821–1921*, p. 7.
7 Ibid., p. 8.
8 Ibid., p. 9; also see the relevant chapters in Kozharinov, *Russian Perfumery*.
9 Lobkovich, *Zolotoy vek russkoy parfyumerii i kosmetiki 1821–1921*, p. 10. Also see the anniversary

publication *Zolotoy yubiley parfyumernogo proizvodstva Tovarishchestva Brokar i Ko v Moskve.*

10 Regarding the most important companies, see Kozharinov, *Russian Perfumery.*

11 Lobkovich, *Zolotoy vek russkoy parfyumerii i kosmetiki 1821–1921*, p. 15.

12 A trove of advertising images can be found in Kozharinov, *Russian Perfumery.*

13 Weriguine, *Souvenirs et parfums* (subsequently published in Russian as Verigin, *Blagoukhannost'*).

14 Weriguine, *Souvenirs et parfums.*

15 Mikhail Loskutov, 'Grazhdanin frantsuzskoy respubliki' ('Citizen of the French Republic'); Dolgopolova, *Parfyumeriya v SSSR*, I, pp. 325f.

16 Regarding Verigin's biography, see the Russian Wikipedia page, https://ru.wikipedia.org/wiki/ Веригин,_Сергий_Константинович.

17 Hans J. Rindisbacher, *The Smell of Books.*

18 Verigin, *Blagoukhannost'*, p. 9.

19 'No odin yest' v mire zapakh, / I odna yest' v mire nega: / Eto russkiy zimniy polden', / Eto russkiy zapakh snega.'

20 Verigin, *Blagoukhannost'*, p. 6.

21 Review of Verigin's memoirs by Olga Kushlina, 'Tumany i dukhi', pp. 81f.; also see Verigin, *Blagoukhannost'*.

22 Kushlina, 'Tumany i dukhi', p. 81; also see Douglas Smith, *Former People.*

23 Olga Vainshtein, *Aromaty i zapakhi v kul'ture*, two volumes; see the essay 'Semiotika "Shanel' No 5"' in volume II.

24 'Olfactory class struggle' can be found in Jan Plamper, 'Sounds of February, Smells of October', a contribution to the 'Centenary Perspectives on the Russian Revolution' conference at the Davis Center, Harvard University, 2017. I would like to thank the author for sharing his unpublished manuscript

with me. Also see Jan Plamper, 'Die Russische Revolution'.

25 See the chapter 'Kommunalka oder Wo der Sowjetmensch gehärtet wurde', in Schlögel, *Das sowjetische Jahrhundert*, pp. 324–45.

26 Stephen Kotkin, *Stalin*, vol. II: *Waiting for Hitler*, p. 124.

27 Regarding inflammatory hate speeches, see Karl Schlögel, *Moscow, 1937*, pp. 68–80.

28 Regarding the *vydvizhentsy* ('the promoted') of the 1930s, see Sheila Fitzpatrick, 'Stalin and the Making of a New Elite, 1928–1939'; regarding the culture of arrivistes in the age of Stalin, see Vera Dunham, *In Stalin's Time*.

29 Regarding the design of the Chanel No. 5 bottle, see Edmonde Charles-Roux, *Chanel*, p. 219.

30 Regarding 'multiple modernities', see Michael David-Fox, *Crossing Borders*. The Lenin quote about creating 'the fundamental requisites of civilization in a different way' can be found in Vladimir Ilyich Lenin, 'Our Revolution'.

Departure from the belle époque and clothes for the New Woman

1 Walter Benjamin, *The Arcades Project*, pp. 63f. (the section on 'Fashion').

2 Alexandre Vassiliev, *Beauty in Exile*.

3 Charles-Roux, *Chanel*, pp. 168f.

4 Ibid., p. 267.

5 Strizhenova, *Soviet Costume and Textiles 1917–1945*, p. 310.

6 Ibid., pp. 310f.

7 Also see the summary in Schlögel, *Das sowjetische Jahrhundert*, in the chapter 'Kleider für den neuen Menschen oder', pp. 607–30.

8 In addition to the many biographies of Gabrielle Chanel, there are a number of excellent film essays in the *Inside Chanel* series, including segments with Karl Lagerfeld and interviews, which are available on YouTube, e.g., 'CHANEL No5 – For the First Time' at www.youtube.com/watch?v=tRQa33dqyxI.

9 For more on Nadezhda Lamanova's biography, see Schlögel, *Das sowjetische Jahrhundert*, pp. 623–6.

10 Charles-Roux, *Chanel*, pp. 41, 45f., 57, 78.

11 Regarding *Le train bleu* and Diaghilev in general, see Jane Pritchard (ed.), *Diaghilev and the Golden Age of the Ballets Russes 1909–1929*.

12 Charles-Roux, *Chanel*, p. 253.

13 Harry Kessler, *Das Tagebuch 1880–1937*, vol. VIII, entry for 24 June 1924.

14 Viktoriya Sevryukova, 'Sovetskoye bel'yo', p. 42.

15 Konstantin Rudnitsky, *Russian and Soviet Theater 1905–1932*.

16 Regarding the expo of 1925, see Frank Scarlett and Marjorie Townley, *Arts Décoratifs*; Charlotte Benton et el., *Art Deco*, catalogue of the exhibition on display at the Victoria & Albert Museum from 27 March to 20 July 2003; Axel Madsen, *Sonia Delaunay*; regarding the Russian exhibition, see http://wiki-org.ru/wiki/Всемирная_выставка_ (1925).

17 Charles-Roux, *Chanel*, p. 266; see also Strizhenova, *Soviet Costume and Textiles*, pp. 97–132.

18 Charles-Roux, *Chanel*, p. 267.

Chanel's Russian connection

1 Zweig, *The World of Yesterday*.

2 Benjamin, *The Arcades Project*, as well as Patrice Higonnet, *Paris*.

3 For an account of Paris in the 1920s, see, e.g., Ernest Hemingway, *A Moveable Feast*.
4 Regarding the Nord Express, see Jan Musekamp, 'From Paris to St Petersburg'.
5 Ilya Ehrenburg, *Memoirs*; Ilya Ehrenburg and El Lissitzky, *My Paris*; *Paris–Moscou 1900–1930*, catalogue of the exhibition held at the Centre Pompidou in 1979; Vita Susak, *Ukrainian Artists in Paris 1900–1939*.
6 The film *Coco Chanel & Igor Stravinsky*, directed by Jan Kounen, was based on the novel *Coco and Igor* by Chris Greenhalgh and premiered in Cannes in 2009.
7 Gold and Fizdale, *Misia*; Pritchard (ed.), *Diaghilev and the Golden Age of the Ballets Russes*; Richard Buckle, *Diaghilev*.
8 Robert H. Johnston, *New Mecca, New Babylon*; Catherine Gousseff, *L'exil russe*.
9 Kessler, *Das Tagebuch 1880–1937*.
10 Charles-Roux, *Chanel*, p. 225.
11 See Vassiliev, *Beauty in Exile*, pp. 151ff. ('The Kitmir House of Embroidery'); also see Alexandre Vassiliev, *Russkaya moda*.
12 Regarding Shchukin and Morozov's collections, see Költzsch (ed.), *Morozov and Shchukin*, catalogue of the exhibition in Essen, Moscow and Saint Petersburg.

French connection in Moscow?

1 Regarding the internationalism of Moscow in the 1930s, see Katerina Clark, *Moscow, the Fourth Rome*; Michael David-Fox, *Showcasing the Great Experiment*; Ludmila Stern, *Western Intellectuals and the Soviet Union*. I would like to thank Gabor T. Rittersporn for pointing me to the French sympathizers.

2 Paul Vaillant-Couturier, *Les bâtisseurs de la vie nouvelle.*

3 Regarding the competition for the Palace of Soviets, see Karl Schlögel, *Moscow*, pp. 67–81; Selim O. Chan-Magomedov, *Pioniere der sowjetischen Architektur.*

4 André Gide, *Return from the USSR.*

5 Manfred Sapper and Volker Weichsel (eds.), *Der Hitler-Stalin-Pakt.*

6 Mikhail Bulgakov, *The Master and Margarita*, ch. 12.

7 Bulgakov, *The Master and Margarita*, pp. 98f., 105f.

8 It is telling that 'giant' bottles of perfume on a vanity played a role in the denunciation of Mikhail Bulgakov's wife, Yelena Sergeyevna Bulgakova; message from Irina Belobrovtseva, Tallinn.

Auguste Michel's incomplete project

1 See Schlögel, *Moscow, 1937*, specifically the chapter 'Moscow in Paris: The USSR Pavilion at the International Exhibition of 1937', pp. 198–208.

2 Loskutov, 'Grazhdanin frantsuzskoy respubliki'.

3 Regarding the razing of the cathedral, see 'Razrusheniye Khrama Khrista Spasitelya (Samizdat)', London, 1988, as well as the chapter 'The Foundation Pit' in Schlögel, *Moscow, 1937*, pp. 544–57.

4 Quoted in Loskutov, 'Grazhdanin frantsuzskoy respubliki', unpaginated.

5 Djurdja Bartlett, *Fashion East*, pp. 86f.

6 Ibid., pp. 76, 84f.

7 Sergey Zhuravlev and Jukka Gronow, *Fashion Meets Socialism*; Benjamin, *The Arcades Project*, p. 71.

8 According to the database of the human rights organization Memorial, Mikhail Loskutov was arrested on 12 January 1940, sentenced on 6 July 1941 by the Military Collegium of the Supreme Court of the USSR for membership in a terrorist organization, shot on 28 July 1941, and rehabilitated in 1956.

The seductive scent of power

1 Regarding the connection between scent and power, see Classen et al., *Aroma*.
2 For the biography of Zhemchuzhina-Molotova, see Larissa Vasilieva, *Kremlin Wives*, and Boris Morozov, 'Zhemchuzhina, Polina Semenovna'. A short biography can be found in Georgi Dimitrov, *The Diary of Georgi Dimitrov*, pp. 148f. Also see Sheila Fitzpatrick, *On Stalin's Team*; Kotkin, *Stalin*, vol. II: *Waiting for Hitler*; Svetlana Alliluyeva, *Twenty Letters to a Friend*. Online sources are available as well, with information of varying provenance and reliability: www.pseudology.org/evrei/Zhemchuzhina.htm; https://en.wikipedia.org/wiki/Polina_Zhemchuzhina; www.e-reading.club/chapter.php/39547/20/leonid-mlechin-zachem-stalin-sozdal-izrail.html; 'Polina Zhemchuzhina – biografiya, informatsiya, lichnaya zhizn' at http://stuki-druki.dom/authors/Zhemchuzhina-Polina.php; Anna Belova, '"Zhemchuzhina" Vyacheslava Molotova: Supruga narkoma, kotoruyu nenavidel Stalin' at https://kulturologia.ru/blogs/071218/41551.
3 Besides the many biographies of Chanel, there are several good documentaries which include interviews. See the *Inside Chanel* series at https://inside.chanel.com.

4 Hal Vaughan, *Sleeping with the Enemy*.
5 Court records and Sûreté files; see Vaughan, *Sleeping with the Enemy*, pp. 138ff.
6 A picture of the building at 24 Quai de la Béthune that belonged to Helena Rubinstein, which replaced an earlier building demolished in 1934, can be found at https://de.wikipedia.org/wiki/Helena_Rubinstein.
7 Wolfgang Seibel, *Persecution and Rescue*.
8 Ernst Jünger, *A German Officer in Occupied Paris*.
9 Regarding Chanel's battle with the Wertheimers, see Vaughan, *Sleeping with the Enemy*, pp. 147ff.
10 See Vaughan, *Sleeping with the Enemy*, pp. 204ff. Regarding Chanel's return to Paris, see the reprints of articles by Jean Cocteau – e.g., 'Le retour de Mademoiselle Chanel' reprinted in Froment, *No. 5 Culture Chanel*.
11 The information here on Polina Zhemchuzhina has been collated from Vasilieva, *Kremlin Wives*, as well as films on YouTube; 'Polina Zhemchuzhina – biografiya, informatsiya, lichnaya zhizn' at http://stuki-druki.dom/authors/Zhemchuzhina-Polina.php; www.knowbysight.info; https://en.wikipedia.org/wiki/Polina_Zhemchuzhina; and https://ru.m.wikipedia.org/wiki/Жемчужина,_Полина_Семёновна; Fitzpatrick, *On Stalin's Team*, p. 331.
12 'The most prominent Soviet wife, Polina Zhemchuzhina (Molotova), was head of the Soviet perfume and cosmetics industry': Yuri Slezkine, *The House of Government*, p. 622.
13 Alliluyeva, *Twenty Letters to a Friend*, pp. 115f.; regarding Zhemchuzhina's arrest in early 1949, see ibid., p. 63.
14 Zhemchuzhina is mentioned multiple times in Felix Chuev, *Sto sorok besed s Molotovym* (and in the abridged English version published as *Molotov Remembers*).
15 See the analysis by Zhores Medvedev (in Medvedev

and Roy A. Medvedev, *The Unknown Stalin*), as well as Delo Yevreyskogo Antifashistskogo Komiteta, 'Dokument No 2'; Delo Yevreyskogo Antifashistskogo Komiteta, 'Dokument No 14'.

16 Regarding correspondence between Jewish Soviet citizens and their relatives abroad in this period, see Leonid I. Smilovitsky, 'Jews from the USSR Write Abroad'.

17 Joseph E. Davies, *Mission to Moscow*, p. 83 (entry from 14 March 1937).

18 Ibid., pp. 83f.

19 Ibid., p. 275.

20 Slezkine, *The House of Government*, pp. 550f. For more on Alexander Arosev (1890–1938), an urbane diplomat and writer, key figure in Soviet cultural diplomacy and victim of the purges, see David-Fox, *Showcasing the Great Experiment*.

21 See Hans Rogger, 'Amerikanizm and the Economic Development of Russia'.

22 Regarding the interrogations, see Vyacheslav Nikonov, *Molotov*, pp. 19f.; Delo Yevreyskogo Antifashistskogo Komiteta, 'Dokument No 2'.

23 Nikonov, *Molotov*, p. 20.

24 Dimitrov, *The Diary of Georgi Dimitrov*, p. 149; also see Nikonov, *Molotov*, p. 76.

25 Kotkin, *Stalin*, vol. II: *Waiting for Hitler*, p. 692; Oleg Khlevniuk, *Master of the House*, pp. 219f.

26 Vasilieva, *Kremlin Wives*, p. 144. I have not found any information about a trip abroad in 1924, but there is evidence of a trip to the USA in 1946 in connection with the Jewish Anti-Fascist Committee.

27 English version: Ilya Ehrenburg and Vasily Grossman, *The Complete Black Book of Russian Jewry*.

28 Golda Meir, *My Life*, pp. 253f.

29 Delo Yevreyskogo Antifashistskogo Komiteta, 'Document No 14'.

30 Regarding antisemitism in the late Stalin era, see Frank Grüner, *Patrioten und Kosmopoliten*.

31 The phrase 'iron woman' (*zheleznaia zhenshchina*) refers to a documentary novel by Nina Berberova, published in English as *Moura*.

32 Vasilieva, *Kremlin Wives*, p. 159.

33 Fitzpatrick, *On Stalin's Team*, pp. 204–8.

34 Louis Rapoport, *Stalin's War Against the Jews*.

35 Regarding the 'anti-cosmopolitan' and 'anti-Zionist' campaign, see Gennadi Kostyrchenko, *Stalin protiv 'kosmopolitov'*; Arno Lustiger, *Stalin and the Jews*; for the biography of Lina Stern, see www.sakharov-center.ru/asfcd/auth/?t=author & i=1484.

36 Molotov frequently mentioned the need to eliminate 'fifth columns'; see Chuev, *Sto sorok besed s Molotovym*, pp. 390, 428 (also see Chuev, *Molotov Remembers*, pp. 160, 254).

37 See the many references in Nikonov, *Molotov*; here, p. 264.

38 Chuev, *Sto sorok besed s Molotovym*, p. 173 (also see Chuev, *Molotov Remembers*, p. 417).

39 Cocteau, 'Le retour de Mademoiselle Chanel'.

From another world

1 Regarding the shooting procedure in Butovo and Kommunarka, see Schlögel, *Moscow, 1937*, pp. 483f.

2 Rindisbacher, *The Smell of Books*; Ekaterina Zhiritskaya, 'Zapakh Kolymy'.

3 Quoted in Rindisbacher, *The Smell of Books*, p. 260.

4 Rudolf Hoess, *Commandant of Auschwitz*, pp. 154, 190f.

5 See Rindisbacher, *The Smell of Books*, pp. 239ff.

6 Olga Lengyel, *Five Chimneys* (1947), quoted in Rindisbacher, *The Smell of Books*, pp. 242f.

7 Primo Levi, *Survival in Auschwitz and The Reawakening* (1986), quoted in Rindisbacher, *The Smell of Books*, p. 244.
8 Zhiritskaya, 'Zapakh Kolymy'; Varlam Shalamov, *Kolyma Tales*.
9 Zhiritskaya, 'Zapakh Kolymy'.

After the war

1 See Natalya Dolgopolova, *Parfyumeriya v SSSR*, II, p. 16.
2 Regarding the period known as the Thaw, see Ilya Ehrenburg, *The Thaw*; Sergei Zhuk, *Rock and Roll in the Rocket City*; catalogue and materials relating to the outstanding 'Ottepel' exhibition held at the State Tretyakov Gallery in Moscow in 2017.
3 Schlögel, *Das sowjetische Jahrhundert*, pp. 608–12.
4 Regarding the individual masters, see Dolgopolova, *Parfyumeriya v SSSR*, II, pp. 310–24; Melodii Trav, 'Istoriya parfyumerii. Chast', 3: Flakony'.
5 Dolgopolova, *Parfyumeriya v SSSR*, II, p. 167.
6 Ibid., p. 121.
7 Ibid., p. 169.
8 Quoted in Dolgopolova, *Parfyumeriya v SSSR*, II, p. 113; Eleonory Gilburd, *To See Paris and Die*.
9 Dolgopolova, *Parfyumeriya v SSSR*, II, p. 14.
10 Ibid., pp. 6, 25.
11 A lively debate surrounds the authorship and genesis of Red Poppy, the Soviet equivalent to Opium; Roland Barthes, 'The Match between Chanel and Vourrèges as Refereed by a Philosopher'.
12 Dolgopolova, *Parfyumeriya v SSSR*, II, p. 104.
13 Information compiled from articles by Alexei Polikovskiy, 'Parfyum "Pulya v zatylok"', *Novaya Gazeta*, 30 October 2019, https://novayagazeta. ru/articles/2019/10/30/82556-parfyum-pulya-v-zaty

lok; Konstantin Mikhailov, 'Rasstrel'nyy butik na
Nikol'skoy', *Kommersant*, 2 July 2018, www.kom
mersant.ru/doc/3656607; 'Petitsiya "Novoy" protiv
otkrytiya butika v Rasstrel'nom Dome podpisali
30 tysyach chelovek', *Novaya Gazeta*, 4 November
2019, https://novayagazeta.ru/news/2019/11/04/15
6630-petitsiyu-novoy-protiv-otkrytiya-butika-v-ra
sstrelnom-dome-podpisali-30-tysyach-chelovek;
Yuriy Biryukov, 'Istoriya "Rasstrel'nogo doma"
na Nikol'skoy', 9 January 2012, https://archn
adzor-ru.livejournal.com/259762.html; for cover-
age in English, see https://uk.reuters.com/article/uk
-russia-stalin-terror-perfume/activists-make-sce
nt-of-fear-to-protest-perfumery-at-soviet-purge-
site-idUKKBN20X2JV, and www.cbc.ca/radio/as
ithappens/as-it-happens-wednesday-edition-1.54
85533/ad-agency-makes-death-sentence-fragrance-
to-protest-perfume-shop-in-stalin-execution-ho
use-1.5485535.

Excursus

1 For the history of the UFA film company, see Klaus
Kreimeier, *The Ufa Story*.
2 Regarding the history of the Chekhov family, see
Renate Helker, *Die Tschechows*, which includes a
family tree of the 'clan'.
3 Regarding Chekhova's entanglements, see the well-
researched and scrupulous book by Antony Beevor,
The Mystery of Olga Chekhova; also see Maya
Turovskaya, 'Shpionka Stalina ili konfidentka
Gitlera'; Mark Kushnirov, *Ol'ga Chekhova*; Nikolai
Dolgopolov, 'Neizvestnaya rol' Ol'gi Chekhovoy'.
4 Olga Tschechowa [Chekhova], *Meine Uhren gehen
anders*, p. 253.
5 Tschechowa, *Meine Uhren gehen anders*, p. 253.

Kushnirov rightly points out that the meeting with the professor is more likely to have taken place in Paris than London.

6 The perfumes created by Olga Chekhova can be found at www.parfumo.net/Perfumes/Olga_ Tschechowa.

7 Olga Tschechowa, *Plauderei über die Schönheit*; Olga Tschechowa and Günter René Evers, *Frau ohne Alter*.

8 Tschechowa and Evers, *Frau ohne Alter*, pp. 337, 339.

9 Tschechowa, *Plauderei über die Schönheit*, pp. 43f., 46.

10 Website of the Académie Scientifique de Beauté at www.academiebeaute.com/en/the-brand/history. html.

11 Alexander A. Bogomolets, *The Prolongation of Life*; an appraisal of Bogomolets's scientific achievements can be found in Yuriy Vilenskiy, 'Nauchnoye naslediye akademika A. A. Bogomol'tsa'; a biography can be found at https://ru.wikipedia.org/ wiki/Богомолец,_Александр_Александрович, and a briefer overiew at https://en.wikipedia.org/wiki/ Aleksandr_Bogomolets.

12 Michael Hagemeister, '"Unser Körper muss unser Werk sein"'.

How One World smells

1 Regarding the 'changed Moscow', see Schlögel, *Moskau lesen*, pp. 347–467.

2 Regarding shopping tourism, bazaars and the creeping currents of informal trade, see Karl Schlögel, 'Archipelago Europe'.

3 Gianluigi Guido, 'The Luxury Fashion Market in Russia'.

4 Moritz Gathmann, 'Lagerfelds Mode für Moskau'.
5 Karl Schlögel, 'Die Farbe der Globalisierung'.

Not only the Black Square

1 Alexandra Shatskikh, 'Flakon Malevicha'; Sergey Borisov, 'Famous Artists as Perfume Bottle and Packaging Designers'; Jillian Steinhauer, 'Kazimir Malevich's Little-Known Perfume Bottle'; Dolgopolova, *Parfyumeriya v SSSR*, I, p. 109.
2 Regarding Malevich's work, see Larissa A. Zhadova, *Malevich*.
3 Numerous images of the polar bear bottle and advertising posters can be found in Aleksandra Shatskikh's article 'Flakon Malevicha'.
4 The Cubo-Futurist paintings *Vanity Case* from 1913 and *Knife Grinder* from 1912–13 can be found in *Kazimir Malevich 1878–1935*, the catalogue of the exhibition shown in Leningrad, Moscow and Amsterdam 1988–9, pp. 80, 93.
5 Shatskikh, 'Flakon Malevicha'; Christiane Bauermeister et al., *Sieg über die Sonne*.
6 Mikhail Vodopyanov, *Die Eroberung des Nordpols*; also see Schlögel, *Moscow, 1937*, pp. 274–93.
7 Borisov, 'Famous Artists as Perfume Bottle and Packaging Designers'; Philip Goutell, 'Perfume Projects'; regarding *shtof* as a liquid measure and vodka bottle, see Geneviève Delafon, 'Rives, le Dauphiné et la Russie', and the entry in the *Entsiklopedicheskiy slovar' Brokgauza i Yefrona*, LXXVIII, p. 921.

Bibliography

Académie Scientifique de beauté, www.academiebeaute.
com/en/the-brand/history.html.

Alliluyeva, Svetlana, *Twenty Letters to a Friend*, translated by Priscilla Johnson, London: Hutchinson, 1967 [*Dvadtsat' pisem k drugu*, 1967].

Antonova, Irina, et al., *Chanel: l'art comme univers*, Moscow: Pushkin Museum, 2007.

'Aromaty sovetskoy zhenshchiny', *Back in the USSR*, May 2015, http://back-in-ussr.com/2015/05/aroma ty-sovetskoy zhenschiny.html.

Avetisyan, Roxana, 'Minpromtorg izuchayet vozmozhnost' importozameshcheniya v parfyumerii', *Izvestia*, 29 August 2017, https://iz.ru/634495/roksana-aveti sian/minpromtorg-zadumalsia-ob-importozamesh chenii-kosmetiki-i-dukhov.

Barthes, Roland, 'The Match between Chanel and Vourrèges as Refereed by a Philosopher', *Marie Claire*, September 1967, reprinted in Froment, *No. 5 Culture Chanel*, pp. 43–4.

Bartlett, Djurdja, *Fashion East: The Spectre That Haunted Socialism*, Cambridge, MA: MIT Press, 2010.

Bauermeister, Christiane, et al., *Sieg über die Sonne: Aspekte russischer Kunst zu Beginn des 20. Jahrhunderts*, Berlin: Fröhlich & Kaufmann, 1983.

Beevor, Antony, *The Mystery of Olga Chekhova*, London: Penguin, 2004.

Beil, Ralf (ed.), *Russland 1900: Kunst und Kultur im Reich des letzten Zaren*, Cologne: DuMont, 2008.

Belova, Anna, '"Zhemchuzhina" Vyacheslava Molotova: Supruga narkoma, kotoruyu nenavidel Stalin', *Kulturologia.ru*, 7 December 2018, https://kulturo logia.ru/blogs/071218/41551.

Benjamin, Walter, *The Arcades Project*, translated by Howard Eiland and Kevin McLaughlin, Cambridge, MA: Harvard University Press, 1999 [*Das Passagen-Werk* in *Gesammelte Schriften*, vol. V].

Benton, Charlotte, Tim Benton, and Ghislaine Wood (eds), *Art Deco: 1910–1939*, London: V&A Publishing, 2003.

Berberova, Nina, *Moura: The Dangerous Life of the Baroness Budberg*, translated by Marian Schwartz and Richard D. Sylvester, New York Review of Books, 2005 [*Zheleznaia Zhenshchina*, 1988].

Bogomolets, Alexander A., *The Prolongation of Life*, translated by Peter V. Karpovich and Sonia Bleeker, New York: Duell, Sloan & Pearce, 1946 [*Prodlenie zhizni*, 1940].

Borisov, Sergey, 'Famous Artists as Perfume Bottle and Packaging Designers', www.fragrantica.com/news/ Famous-Artists-as-Perfume-Bottle-and-Packaging-Designers-10473.html.

Bortschagowski, Alexander, *Orden für einen Mord: Die Judenverfolgung unter Stalin*, translated by Alfred Frank, Berlin: Propyläen, 1997.

Buckle, Richard, *Diaghilev*, New York: Atheneum, 1979.

Bulgakov, Mikhail, *The Master and Margarita*, translated by Diana Burgin and Katherine Tiernan O'Connor, London: Picador, 1997 [*Master i Margarita*, 1966].

Chan-Magomedov, Selim O., *Pioniere der sowjetischen Architektur: Der Weg zur neuen sowjetischen*

Architektur in den zwanziger und zu Beginn der dreißiger Jahre, Dresden: VEB Verlag der Kunst, 1983.

Charles-Roux, Edmonde, *Chanel: Her Life, Her World, and the Woman Behind the Legend She Herself Created*, translated by Nancy Amphoux, London: MacLehose Press, 2009 [1975] [*L'Irrégulière ou mon itinéraire Chanel*, 1974].

Charles-Roux, Edmonde, *Chanel and Her World: Friends, Fashion, and Fame*, translated by Daniel Wheeler, New York: Vendome Press, 2005 [*Le temps Chanel*, 1979].

Chuev, Felix, *Sto sorok besed s Molotovym: Iz dnevnika F. Chueva*, Moscow: Terra, 1991, http://stalinism.ru/elektronnaya-biblioteka/sto-sorok-besed-s-molotovyim.html [abridged English version published as *Molotov Remembers: Inside Kremlin Politics*, 1993].

Clark, Katerina, *Moscow, the Fourth Rome: Stalinism, Cosmopolitanism and the Evolution of Soviet Culture, 1931–1941*, Cambridge, MA: Harvard University Press, 2011.

Classen, Constance, David Howes and Anthony Synnott, *Aroma: The Cultural History of Smell*, London: Routledge, 1994.

Cocteau, Jean, 'Le retour de Mademoiselle Chanel', *Femina*, March 1954, reprinted in Froment, *No. 5 Culture Chanel*, p. 5.

Corbin, Alain, *The Foul and the Fragrant: Odor and the French Social Imagination*, translated by Miriam L. Kochan with Dr Roy Porter and Christopher Prendergast, Cambridge, MA: Harvard University Press, 1986 [*Le miasme et la jonquille*, 1982].

David-Fox, Michael, *Crossing Borders: Modernity, Ideology, and Culture in Russia and the Soviet Union*, University of Pittsburgh Press, 2015.

David-Fox, Michael, *Showcasing the Great Experiment: Cultural Diplomacy and Western Visitors to the*

Soviet Union 1921–1941, Oxford University Press, 2012.

Davies, Joseph E., *Mission to Moscow*, London: Victor Gollancz Limited, 1945.

Davydov, Aleksandr Y., *Meshochniki i diktatura v Rossii 1917–1921*, Saint Petersburg: Aleteia, 2007.

Delafon, Geneviève, 'Rives, le Dauphiné et la Russie, Alphonse Rallet, parfumeur des tsars', *Les Chroniques: Revue d'Histoire en Dauphiné*, 62, December 2016, pp. 36–41.

Delo Yevreyskogo Antifashistskogo Komiteta, 'Dokument No 2: Zapiska M. F. Shkiryatova i V. S. Abakumova o P. S. Zhemchuzhnoy', 27 December 1948, in RGASPI. f. 589, op. 3, d. 6188, l. 25–31, www.alexanderyakovlev.org/almanah/inside/almanah-doc/79.

Delo Yevreyskogo Antifashistskogo Komiteta, 'Dokument No 14: L. P. Beriya – v prezidium TSK KPSS o rezul'tatakh izucheniya obstoyatel'stv aresta i osuzhdeniya P. S. Zhemchuzhinoy', 5 December 1953, in AP RF, f. 3., op. 32, d. 17, l. 131–4, www.alexanderyakovlev.org/fond/issues-doc/68504.

Dimitrov, Georgi, *The Diary of Georgi Dimitrov, 1933–1949*, edited by Ivo Banac, translated by Jane T. Hedges, Timothy D. Sergay and Irina Faion, New Haven and London: Yale University Press, 2003 [*Dnevnik*, 1997].

Dolgopolov, Nikolai, 'Neizvestnaya rol' Ol'gi Chekhovoy', *Rodina*, 6 (616), 1 June 2016, https://rg.ru/2016/06/09/rodina-chechova.html.

Dolgopolova, Natalya, *Parfyumeriya v SSSR: Obzor i lichnye vpechatleniia kollektsionera*. vol. I, Moscow: Galart, 2016.

Dolgopolova, Nataliia, *Parfyumeriya v SSSR: Obzor i lichnye vpechatleniia kollektsionera*, vol. II, Moscow: Galart, 2018.

Döring, Jürgen (ed.), *Parfum: Ästhetik und Verführung*,

Munich: Prestel, 2005 (to accompany the exhibition at the Museum für Kunst und Gewerbe Hamburg 2005).

Dudintsev, Vladimir, *Not by Bread Alone*, translated by Edith Bone, London: Hutchinson, 1957 [*Ne khlebom yedinym*, 1956].

Dunham, Vera, *In Stalin's Time: Middleclass Values in Soviet Fiction*, Durham, NC, and London: Duke University Press, 1990 [1976].

Edwards, Michael, *Perfume Legends: French Feminine Fragrances*, Levallois: H. M. Editions, 1996.

Ehrenburg, Ilya, *Memoirs: 1921–1941*, translated by Tatania Shebunina in collaboration with Yvonne Kapp, Cleveland: World Publishing Company, 1964 [*Lyudi, gody, zhizn*, 1961].

Ehrenburg, Ilya, *The Thaw*, translated by Manya Harari, London: Harvill, 1955 [*Ottepel*, 1954].

Ehrenburg, Ilya, and Vasily Grossman, *The Complete Black Book of Russian Jewry*, edited and translated by David Patterson, New Brunswick and London: Transaction Publishers, 2002 [*Chiornaya Kniga*, 1946].

Ehrenburg, Ilya, and El Lissitzky, *My Paris*, translated by Oliver Ready, Paris: Edition 7, 2005 [*Moi Parizh*, 1933].

Entsiklopedicheskiy slovar' Brokgauza i Yefrona, vol. LXXVIII, Saint Petersburg: Brockhaus-Efron, 1903.

Ermilova, Daria, 'Sovetskaya moda', in Zuseva (ed.), *Sovetskiy stil'*, pp. 10–37.

Fitzpatrick, Sheila, *On Stalin's Team: The Years of Living Dangerously in Soviet Politics*, Princeton University Press, 2015.

Fitzpatrick, Sheila, 'Stalin and the Making of a New Elite, 1928–1939', *Slavic Review*, 38 (3), 1979, pp. 377–402.

Flanner, Janet, 'Perfume and Politics', *The New*

Yorker, 3 May 1930, www.newyorker.com/maga
zine/1930/05/03/perfume-and-politics.
Fridman, R. A., *Tekhnologiya parfyumerii*, Moscow,
1949.
Froment, Jean-Louis, *No. 5 Culture Chanel*, New York:
Abrams, 2013.
Gathmann, Moritz, 'Lagerfelds Mode für Moskau: Ein
Hauch zu viel', 31 May 2009, www.spiegel.de/pano
rama/leute/lagerfelds-mode-fuer-moskau-ein-hauch-
zu-viel-a-627876.html.
Gide, André, *Return from the USSR*, translated by
Dorothy Bussy, New York: Alfred A. Knopf, 1937
[*Retour de l'U.R.S.S.*, 1936].
Gilburd, Eleonory, *To See Paris and Die: The Soviet
Lives of Western Culture*, Cambridge, MA: Harvard
University Press, 2018.
Gold, Arthur, and Robert Fizdale, *Misia: The Life of
Misia Sert*, New York: Alfred A. Knopf, 1980.
Gousseff, Catherine, *L'exil russe: La fabrique du réfugié
apatride*, Paris: CNRS Editions, 2008.
Goutell, Philip, 'Perfume Projects: Museum of Modern
Perfume', www.perfumeprojects.com/museum/
Museum.shtml.
Grasse: L'usine à parfums. Lyon: Lieux Dits, 2015.
Green, Annette, and Linda Dyett, *Secrets of Aromatic
Jewelry*, Paris and New York: Flammarion, 1998.
Gronow, Jukka, *Caviar with Champagne: Common
Luxury and the Ideals of the Good Life in Stalin's
Russia*, Oxford and New York: Berg, 2003.
Grüner, Frank, *Patrioten und Kosmopoliten: Juden im
Sowjetstaat 1941–1953*, Cologne: Böhlau, 2008.
Guido, Gianluigi, 'The Luxury Fashion Market in
Russia', in Alessandra Vecchi and Chitra Buckley
(eds.), *Handbook of Research on Global Fashion
Management and Merchandising*, Hershey, PA: IGI
Global, 2016, pp. 670–94.
Gurova, Olga, *Sovetskoye nizhneye bel'ye: mezhdu*

ideologiyey i povsednevnost'yu, Moscow: Novoye Literaturnoye Obozreniye, 2008.

Hagemeister, Michael, '"Unser Körper muss unser Werk sein": Beherrschung der Natur und Überwindung des Todes in russischen Projekten des frühen 20. Jahrhunderts', in Boris Groys and Michael Hagemeister (eds.), *Die Neue Menschheit: Biopolitische Utopien in Russland zu Beginn des 20. Jahrhunderts*, Frankfurt: Suhrkamp, 2005, pp. 19–67.

Harms, Ingeborg, 'Chanel: Der Geist des Dufts', *Die Zeit*, 2 May 2013.

Harrison, Marlen Elliot, Eugeniya Chudakova and Julietta Ptoyan, 'Exploring Russian Fragrance History', 8 October 2016, www.fragrantica.com/news/Exploring-Russian-Fragrance-History-8358.html.

Hegel, Georg Wilhelm Friedrich, *Phenomenology of Spirit*, translated by A. V. Miller, Oxford University Press, 1977 [*Phänomenologie des Geistes*, 1807].

Helker, Renata, *Die Tschechows: Wege in die Moderne*, Berlin: Henschel, 2005.

Hemingway, Ernest, *A Moveable Feast*, New York: Charles Scribner's Sons, 1964.

Higonnet, Patrice, *Paris: Capital of the World*, translated by Arthur Goldhammer, Cambridge, MA: Belknap Press of Harvard University Press, 2005 [*Paris, capitale du monde*, 2005].

Hildermeier, Manfred, *Geschichte der Sowjetunion*, Munich: Beck, 1998.

Hillier, Bevis, and Stephen Escritt, *Art Deco Style*, New York: Phaidon, 1997.

Hobsbawm, Eric J., *The Age of Extremes: The Short Twentieth Century, 1914–1991*, London: Michael Joseph, 1994.

Hoess, Rudolf, *Commandant of Auschwitz: The Autobiography of Rudolf Hoess*, translated by Constantine FitzGibbon, London: Phoenix

Press, 2000 [1959] [*Kommandant in Auschwitz: Autobiographische Aufzeichnungen*, 1958].

Huber, Elena, *Mode in der Sowjetunion 1917–1953*, Vienna: Praesens, 2011.

Iosselson, Hugo G., *Spravochnik proizvodstvennika parfyumera*, 1933.

Jellinek, Paul, *Die psychologischen Grundlagen der Parfümerie*, Heidelberg: Hüthig, 1994.

Johnston, Robert H., *New Mecca, New Babylon: Paris and the Russian Exiles, 1920–1945*, Montreal: McGill-Queen's University Press, 1988.

Jones, Geoffrey, *Beauty Imagined: A History of the Global Beauty Industry*, Oxford University Press, 2010.

Jünger, Ernst, *A German Officer in Occupied Paris: The War Journals, 1941–1945*, translated by Thomas S. Hansen and Abby J. Hansen, New York: Columbia University Press, 2019 [*Strahlungen: Das erste Pariser Tagebuch, Kaukasische Aufzeichnungen, Das zweite Pariser Tagebuch, Kirchhorster Blätter*, 1949/1979].

Kabakova, Galina, 'Zapakh Smerti – Geruch des Todes', *Slavjanovedenie*, 6, 2000, pp. 21–5.

Kabakova, Galina, 'Zapakhi v russkoy kul'ture', *Zhivaya starina*, 2, 1998, pp. 36–8.

Kant, Immanuel, *Anthropology from a Pragmatic Point of View*, edited and translated by Robert B. Louden, Cambridge University Press, 2006 [*Anthropologie in pragmatischer Absicht*, 1798].

Kasparov, Gennady N., *Parfyumerno-kosmeticheskoye proizvodstvo*, Moscow: Agropromizdat, 1989.

Kastner, Jeffrey, 'The Art of Scent: 1889–2012', *Artforum International*, 2013.

Kazimir Malevich 1878–1935, catalogue of the exhibition in Leningrad, Moscow and Amsterdam 1988–9, Amsterdam: Stedelijk Museum, 1988.

Kessler, Harry Graf, *Das Tagebuch 1880–1937*, vol. III: *1923–1926*, Stuttgart: Klett-Cotta, 2009.

Khlevniuk, Oleg V., *Master of the House: Stalin and His Inner Circle*, translated by Nora Seligman Favorov, New Haven and London: Yale University Press, 2009 [revised and translated version of *Politbiuro: Mekhanizmy politicheskoi vlasti v 1930-e gody*, 1996].

Koleva, Marina, 'Sovetskaya parfyumeriya' in Zuseva (ed.), *Sovetskiy stil*, pp. 74–85.

Költzsch, Georg-W. (ed.), *Morozov and Shchukin – The Russian Collectors: Monet to Picasso*, translated by Eileen Martin, Cologne: DuMont, 1993 [*Morosow und Schtschukin, die russischen Sammler*, 1993].

Kostyrchenko, Gennadi, *Stalin protiv 'kosmopolitov': Vlast' i evreyskaya intelligentsiya v SSSR*, Moscow: Rosspen, 2009.

Kotkin, Stephen, *Stalin*, vol. II: *Waiting for Hitler, 1928–1941*, London: Allen Lane, 2017.

Kozharinov Veniamin, *Russian Perfumery, 19th and Early 20th Centuries*, Moscow: Sovetsky Sport, 1998.

Kozharinov, Veniamin, *Tvorets illyuzii: Korol' russkoy parfyumerii Genrikh Brokar*, Moscow: Sectoral Bulletins, 2011.

Kraft, Philip, Christine Ledard and Philip Goutell, 'From Rallet No. 1 to Chanel No. 5 versus Mademoiselle Chanel No. 1', *Perfumer&Flavorist*, 32, October 2007, pp. 36–48.

'Krasnaya Moskva', in 'Encyclopedia of Fashion', *Casual*, www.casual-info.ru/wiki/Красная Москва.

'Krasnaya Moskva', Russian Wikipedia, https://ru.wikipedia.org/wiki/Красная_Москва.

Kreimeier, Klaus, *The Ufa Story: A History of Germany's Greatest Film Company, 1918–1945*, translated by Robert Kimber and Rita Kimber, Berkeley: University of California Press, 1999 [*Die Ufa-Story: Geschichte eines Filmkonzerns*, 1992].

Kronhaus, R., 'Alfavit Obonyaniya', *Technika Molodezhi*, 8, 1936, pp. 27–31.

Kushlina, Olga, 'Ot slova k zapakhu: Russkaya litera-
tura, prochitannaya nosom', *NLO*, 3 (43), 2000.
Kushlina, Olga, 'Tumany i dukhi', review of
Blagoukhannost': *Vospominaniya Parfyumera* by
Konstantin Verigin, *NLO*, 3 (43), 2000.
Kushnirov, Mark, *Ol'ga Chekhova*, Moscow: Molodaya
gvardiya, 2015.
Lagerfeld, Karl, *Chanel's Russian Connection*, Steidl:
Göttingen, 2009.
Laukenmann, Joachim, 'Es riecht nach Remake:
Chanel No 5 ist aus einem gefloppten russischen
Parfum entstanden', *SonntagsZeitung*, 30 September
2007.
Lebina, Natalya, *Sovetskaya povsednevnost'*: *Normy i
anomalii. Ot voyennogo kommunizma k bol'shomu
stilyu*, Moscow: Novoye literaturnoye obozreniye,
2015.
Lefkowith, Christie Mayer, *The Art of Perfume:
Discovering and Collecting Perfume Bottles*, New
York: Thames and Hudson, 1994.
Lelièvre, Marie-Dominique, *Le No 5 de Chanel:
Biographie non autorisée*, Paris: Stock, 2020.
Lenin, Vladimir Ilyich, 'The Development of Capitalism
in Russia: The Process of the Formation of the Home
Market for Large-Scale Industry', in *Collected Works*,
vol. III: *The Development of Capitalism in Russia*,
Moscow: Progress Publishers, 1964, pp. 21–608
[*Razvitiye kapitalizma v Rossii*, 1899].
Lenin, Vladimir Ilyich, 'Our Revolution', in *Collected
Works*, vol. XXXIII: *August 1921–March 1923*,
translated and edited by David Skvirsky and George
Hanna, Moscow: Progress Publishers, 1973, pp.
476–80 ['Über unsere Revolution', 1923].
Leontiev, Sergei, 'Genial'nyy shirpotreb: Flakon ode-
kolona po eskizu Kazimira Malevicha vypuskali na
Bakhmet'yevskom stekol'nom zavode v Nikol'ske',
Novaya sotsial'naya gazeta, 29, 10 August 2017,

https://penzatrend.ru/index.php/nsg/item/25356-genialnyy-shirpotreb.

Levinson, Alexey, 'Povsyudu chem-to pakhnet', *Logos*, 1 (22), 2000, pp. 24–41.

Liberman, Alexander, *Then: Photographs 1925–1995*, New York: Random House, 1995.

Likhachev, Dmitriy S., *Poeziya sadov: k semantike sadovo-parkovyh stilei. Sad kak tekst*, Moscow: Soglasie, 1998.

Lipman, Masha, 'Fade to Red? Style in the Land of Anti-style', *The New Yorker*, 21 September 1998, pp. 106–13.

Lobkovich, Viktor, *Zolotoy vek russkoy parfyumerii i kosmetiki 1821–1921*, Minsk: Logvinov, 2005.

Loskutov, Mikhail, 'Grazhdanin frantsuzskoy respubliki', *Nashi dostizheniya*, 2, 1937, https://sergmos.livejournal.com/85233.html.

Lustiger, Arno, *Stalin and the Jews: The Red Book – The Tragedy of the Soviet Jews and the Jewish Anti-Fascist Committee*, translated by Mary Beth Friedrich and Todd Bludeau, New York: Enigma Books, 2003 [*Rotbuch: Stalin und die Juden – Die tragische Geschichte des Jüdischen Antifaschistischen Komitees und der sowjetischen Juden*, 1998].

Madsen, Axel, *Coco Chanel: A Biography*, London: Bloomsbury, 2009 (1990).

Madsen, Axel, *Sonia Delaunay: Artist of the Lost Generation*, New York: McGraw-Hill, 1989.

Mankevich, Irina Anatolyevna, *Povsednevnyy Pushkin: poetika obyknovennogo v zhiznetvorchestve russkogo geniya. Kostyum. Zastol'ye. Aromaty i zapakhi*, Saint Petersburg: Aleteia, 2013.

Mazzeo, Tilar J., *The Secret of Chanel No. 5: The Intimate History of the World's Most Famous Perfume*, New York: HarperCollins, 2010.

Medvedev, Zhores A., and Roy A. Medvedev, *The Unknown Stalin*, translated by Ellen Dahrendorf,

London: I. B. Tauris, 2003 [*Neizvestnyi Stalin*, 2001].

Meir, Golda, *My Life*, New York: G. P. Putnam's Sons, 1975.

Melodii Trav, 'Istoriya parfyumerii. Chast' 3: Flakony. Prodolzheniye', www.livemaster.ru/topic/309251-ist oriya-parfyumerii-chast-3-flakony-prodolzhenie.

Mienert, Marion, *Großfürstin Marija Pavlovna: Ein Leben in Zarenreich und Emigration – Vom Wandel aristokratischer Lebensformen im 20. Jahrhundert*, Frankfurt: Peter Lang, 2005.

Millu, Liana, *Smoke over Birkenau*, translated by Lynne Sharon Schwartz, Philadelphia: Jewish Publication Society, 1991 [*Il fumo di Birkenau*, 1986].

Morand, Paul, *The Allure of Chanel*, translated by Euan Cameron, illustrated by Karl Lagerfeld, London: Pushkin Press, 2008 [*L'allure de Chanel*, 1976].

Morozov, Boris, 'Zhemchuzhina, Polina Semenovna', translated by Chaim Chernikov, in *The YIVO Encyclopedia of Jews in Eastern Europe*, 12 November 2010, https://yivoencyclopedia.org/article.aspx/Zhemchuzhina_Polina_Semenovna.

Musekamp, Jan, 'From Paris to St Petersburg and from Kovno to New York: A Cultural History of Transnational Mobility in East Central Europe', post-doctoral thesis at the Faculty of Social and Cultural Sciences of the European University Viadrina, Frankfurt an der Oder, 2016 (forthcoming).

Nazarova, Nina, '"Krasnaya Moskva": kak priduman-nyye do revolyutsii dukhi stali simvolom SSSR', BBC.com, 19 September 2017, www.bbc.com/russian/fea tures-41304033.

Nietzsche, Friedrich, *Ecce Homo: How to Become What You Are*, translated by Duncan Large, Oxford University Press, 2007 [*Ecce Homo*, 1908].

Nietzsche, Friedrich, *Thus Spoke Zarathustra: A Book for All and None*, in *The Portable Nietzsche*, edited and translated by Walter Kaufmann, New York: Penguin Books, 1982, pp. 112–439 [*Also Sprach Zarathustra*, 1883–5].

Nikonov, Vyacheslav, *Molotov: Molodost'*, Moscow: Vagrius, 2005.

Nikonov, Vyacheslav, *Molotov: nashe delo pravoe*, Moscow: Molodaya Gvardiya, 2016.

Obolensky, Igor, *Russkiy sled Koko Shanel'*, Moscow: AST, 2015.

Paris–Moscou 1900–1930, exhibition catalogue, Paris: Centre Georges Pompidou, 1979.

'Perfume: Aromatics Sources', Wikipedia, https://en.wikipedia.org/wiki/Perfume#Aromatics_sources.

Pichyk, N. E., *Bogomolec*, Moscow, 1964.

Pirogovskaya, Maria, *Miazmy, simptomy, uliki: Zapakhi mezhdu meditsinoy i moral'yu v russkoy kul'ture vtoroy poloviny XIX veka*, Saint Petersburg: European University, 2018.

Plamper, Jan, 'Die Russische Revolution: Vier Forschungstrends und ein sinneshistorischer Zugang – mit ausgewählten Quellen für den Geschichtsunterricht', *Geschichte für heute*, 10 (4), 2017, pp. 5–17.

Plamper, Jan, 'Sounds of February, Smells of October: A Sensory History of the Russian Revolution', unpublished manuscript, 2017.

Pritchard, Jane (ed.), *Diaghilev and the Golden Age of the Ballets Russes 1909–1929*, London: V&A Publishing, 2010.

Proust, Marcel, *In Search of Lost Time*, vol. I: *Swann's Way*, translated by C. K. Scott Moncrieff and Terence Kilmartin, revised by D. J. Enright, New York: The Modern Library, 1992.

Quiquempois, Olivier, Valérie Castera, Grégory Couderc, Anne Kraatz and Elise Dubreuil, *De la Belle*

Époque aux Années folles, la parfumerie au tournant du XXe siècle / From the Belle Époque to the Roaring Twenties, Perfumery at the Turn of the Twentieth Century, Nice: Gilletta, 2016.

Raab, Jürgen, *Soziologie des Geruchs: Über die soziale Konstruktion olfaktorischer Wahrnehmung*, Constance: UVK Verlag, 2001.

Rapoport, Louis, *Stalin's War against the Jews: The Doctor's Plot and the Soviet Solution*, New York: The Free Press, 1990.

Raspopina, Sasha, 'Smells Like Soviet Spirit: A Brief History of Perfume and Cosmetics', *The Guardian*, 19 November 2014, www.theguardian.com/world/2014/nov/19/-sp-soviet-makeup-brief-history-russia.

Rogger, Hans, 'Amerikanizm and the Economic Development of Russia', *Comparative Studies in Society and History* 23 (3), July 1981, pp. 382–420.

Reinarz, Jonathan, *Past Scents: Historical Perspectives on Smell*, Urbana: University of Illinois Press, 2014.

Rimmel, Eugène, *The Book of Perfumes*, London: Chapman and Hall, 1867.

Rindisbacher, Hans J., *The Smell of Books: A Cultural-Historical Study of Olfactory Perception in Literature*, Ann Arbor: University of Michigan Press, 1995.

Rubenstein, Joshua, and Vladimir P. Naumov (eds.), *Stalin's Secret Pogrom: The Postwar Inquisition of the Jewish Anti-Fascist Committee*, translated by Laura Esther Wolfson, New Haven: Yale University Press, 2001 [*Nepravednyi Sud*, 1994].

Rudnitsky, Konstantin, *Russian and Soviet Theater 1905–1932*, translated by Roxane Permar, London: Thames and Hudson, 1988.

Sapper, Manfred, and Volker Weichsel (eds.), *Der Hitler-Stalin-Pakt: Der Krieg und die europäische Erinnerung*, Berlin: Berliner Wissenschafts-Verlag, 2009.

Scarlett, Frank, and Marjorie Townley, *Arts Décoratifs:*

A Personal Recollection of the Paris Exhibition 1925, London: Academy Editions, 1975.

Schlögel, Karl, 'Archipelago Europe', translated by John Kerr, *Osteuropa*, Digest 2007: *The Europe Beyond Europe*, pp. 9–36 ['Archipel Europa', in *Marjampole oder Europas Wiederkehr aus dem Geist der Städte*, 2005].

Schlögel, Karl, *Das sowjetische Jahrhundert: Archäologie einer untergegangenen Welt*, Munich: Beck, 2017.

Schlögel, Karl, 'Die Farbe der Globalisierung: Der Vuitton-Koffer auf dem Roten Platz', *Tumult: Vierteljahresschrift für Konsensstörung*, Winter 2014/2015, pp. 29–31.

Schlögel, Karl, *Moscow*, translated by Helen Atkins, London: Reaktion Books, 2005 [abridged translation of *Moskau lesen*, 1984].

Schlögel, Karl, *Moscow, 1937*, translated by Rodney Livingstone, Cambridge: Polity, 2012 [*Terror und Traum: Moskau 1937*, 2008].

Schlögel, Karl, *Moskau lesen: Verwandlungen einer Metropole*, Munich: Carl Hanser, 2011 [1984].

Schopenhauer, Arthur, *The World as Will and Representation*, vol. II, translated by E. F. J. Payne, Indian Hills, CO: The Falcon's Wing Press, 1958 [*Die Welt als Wille und Vorstellung*, 1818–59].

Seibel, Wolfgang, *Persecution and Rescue: The Politics of the 'Final Solution' in France, 1940–1944*, translated by Ciaran Cronin, Ann Arbor: University of Michigan Press, 2016 [*Macht und Moral: Die 'Endlösung der Judenfrage' in Frankreich*, 2010].

Sevryukova, Viktoriya, 'Sovetskoye bel'yo' in Zuseva (ed.), *Sovetskiy stil*, pp. 38–51.

Shalamov, Varlam, *Kolyma Tales*, translated by John Glad, London: Penguin Books, 1994 [*Kolymskiye rasskazy*, 1978].

Shatskikh, Aleksandra, *Black Square: Malevich and the Origin of Suprematism*, translated by Marian

Schwartz, New Haven and London: Yale University Press, 2012 [*Chernyi kvadrat*, 2001].

Shatskikh, Aleksandra, 'Flakon Malevicha: upakovka mechty', *Artguide*, 6 December 2017, http://artguide.com/posts/1382.

Shchipakina, Alla, *Moda v SSSR: Sovetskiy Kuznetskiy 14*, Moscow: Slovo, 2009.

Slezkine, Yuri, *The House of Government: A Saga of the Russian Revolution*, Princeton University Press, 2017.

Slezkine, Yuri, *The Jewish Century*, Princeton University Press, 2019.

Smilovitsky, Leonid I., 'Jews from the USSR Write Abroad (Letters and Diaries of World War II as a Historical Source)', Parts I and II: *Russkii Arkhiv*, 5 (1), 2017, pp. 12–32, and *Russkii Arkhiv*, 5 (2), 2017, pp. 106–24.

Smith, Douglas, *Former People: The Last Days of the Russian Aristocracy*, London: Macmillan, 2012.

Steinhauer, Jillian, 'Kazimir Malevich's Little-Known Perfume Bottle', *Hyperallergic*, 17 July 2014, https://hyperallergic.com/138287/kazimir-malevichs-little-known-perfume-bottle.

Stern, Ludmila, *Western Intellectuals and the Soviet Union, 1920–40: From Red Square to the Left Bank*, New York: Routledge, 2007.

Strizhenova, Tatiana, *Soviet Costume and Textiles 1917–1945*, translated by Era Mozolkova, Paris: Flammarion, 1991 [*Iz istorii sovetskogo kostiuma*, 1972].

Susak, Vita, *Ukrainian Artists in Paris 1900–1939*, translated by Serhiy Synhayivsky and Anna Susak, Kiev: Rodovid Press, 2010 [*Ukrains'ki mysttsi Paryzha: 1900–1939*, 2010].

Süskind, Patrick, *Perfume: The Story of a Murderer*, translated by John E. Woods, New York: Vintage

International, 1986 [*Das Parfum: Die Geschichte eines Mörders*, 1985].

Tietze, Katharina, '"Schönheit für alle": Parfums in der DDR', unpublished manuscript.

Trotsky, Leon, *The Permanent Revolution and Results and Prospects*, translated by John G. Wright and Brian Pearce, London: New Park, 1982 [*Permanentnaya revolyutsiya*, 1930; *Itogi i perspektivy*, 1906].

Tschechowa, Olga [Olga Chekhova], *Meine Uhren gehen anders*, Munich and Berlin: Herbig, 1973.

Tschechowa, Olga [Olga Chekhova], *Plauderei über die Schönheit*, Berlin: Steuben, 1949.

Tschechowa, Olga [Olga Chekhova], and Günter René Evers, *Frau ohne Alter: Schönheits- und Modebrevier*, Munich: Evers, 1952.

Turovskaya, Maya, 'Shpionka Stalina ili konfidentka Gitlera: Kazus Ol'gi Chekhovoy', *Snob*, 12 (77), 14 December 2014, https://snob.ru/magazine/ent ry/84689.

Vaillant-Couturier, Paul, *Les bâtisseurs de la vie nouvelle: neuf mois de voyage dans l'URSS du plan quinquennal*, Paris: Bureau d'Éditions, 1932.

Vainshtein, Olga, *Dendi: Moda, literatura, stil' zhizni*, Moscow: Novoe literaturnoe obozrenie, 2006.

Vainshtein, Olga (ed.), *Aromaty i zapakhi v kul'ture*, vols. I, II, Moscow: Novoe literaturnoe obozrenie, 2003, 2010.

Vasilieva, Larissa, *Kremlin Wives: The Secret Lives of the Women Behind the Kremlin Walls – From Lenin to Gorbachev*, translated by Cathy Porter, New York: Arcade Publishing, 1994 [*Kremlevskie zheny: Fakty, vospominaniia, dokumenty, slukhi, legendy i vzgliad avtora*, 1992].

Vassiliev, Alexandre, *Beauty in Exile: The Artists, Models, and Nobility Who Fled the Russian Revolution and Influenced the World of Fashion*, translated by Antonina W. Bouis and Anya Kucharev,

New York: Harry N. Abrams, 2000 [*Krasota v izgnanii: Tvorchestvo russkikh emigrantov pervoy volny*, 1998].

Vassiliev, Alexandre, *Russkaya moda: 150 let v fotografiyah*, Moscow: Slovo, 2004.

Vaughan, Hal, *Sleeping with the Enemy: Coco Chanel, Nazi Agent*, London: Chatto & Windus, 2011.

Verigin, Konstantin Mikhailovich, *Blagoukhannost': Vospominaniya Parfyumera*, Moscow: Kleograf, 1996, www.e-reading.club/book.php?book=1016413.

Vilenskiy, Yuriy, 'Nauchnoye naslediye akademika A. A. Bogomol'tsa (k 130-letiyu so dnya rozhdeniya)', *Fiziologicheskiy zhurnal*, 57 (3), 2011, pp. 88–95.

Vodopyanov, Mikhail, *Die Eroberung des Nordpols*, London: Malik, 1938.

Weriguine, Constantin, *Souvenirs et parfums: Mémoires d'un parfumeur*, translated by Irène Kalaschnikowa-Brisville, Paris: Plon, 1965 [Konstantin Verigin, *Blagoukhannost': Vospominaniya Parfyumera*, 1996].

Wlasowa, Viktoriya, 'Krasnaya Moskva: The Life of a Legend', 1 December 2018, www.fragrantica.com/news/Krasnaya-Moskva-The-Life-of-a-Legend-11654.html.

Wlasowa, Viktoriya, 'Krasnaya Moskva: Novaya Epokha', 26 November 2018, www.fragrantica.ru/news/Krasnaya-Moskva-novaya-epokha-7725.html.

Wlasowa, Viktoriya, 'Steklyannyy medved' Malevicha – odekolon Severnyy', 7 September 2018, www.fragrantica.ru/news/Steklyannyy-medved-Malevicha-odekolon-Severnyy-7410.html.

Yurova, Elena, 'Ukrasheniye v SSSR', in Zuseva (ed.), *Sovetskiy stil'*, pp. 52–73.

Zellal, Coline, *A l'ombre des usines en fleurs: Genre et travail dans la parfumerie grassoise, 1900–1950*, Aix-en-Provence: Presses universitaires de Provence, 2013.

Zhadova, Larissa A., *Malevich: Suprematism and*

Revolution in Russian Art 1910–1930, translated by Alexander Lieven, London: Thames & Hudson, 1982.

Zhiritskaya, Ekaterina, 'Legkoye dykhaniye: zapakh kak kul'turnaya repressiya v rossiyskom obshchestve 1917–30-kh gg', in Vainshtein (ed.), *Aromaty i zapakhi v kul'ture*, vol. II.

Zhiritskaya, Ekaterina, 'Tumany i dukhi', review of *Blagoukhannost'*: *Vospominaniia Parfiumera*, in *Zapakhi v russkoy kul'ture*, vol. II.

Zhiritskaya, Ekaterina, 'Zapakh Kolymy', *Teoriya mody*, 28, 2013, www.intelros.ru/readroom/teoriya-mody/28-2013/20289-zapah-kolymy.html.

Zhiritskaya, Ekaterina, 'Zapakh rodiny', *Moskovskie novosti*, 12 October 1998.

Zhirnov, Evgeny, 'Pervyy sekret "Shanel' N5"', *Kommersant Dengi*, 40, 15 October 2007, www.kommersant.ru/doc/813950.

Zhuk, Sergei I., *Rock and Roll in the Rocket City: The West, Identity, and Ideology in Soviet Dniepropetrovsk, 1960–1985*, Baltimore, MD: Johns Hopkins University Press, 2010.

Zhuravlev, Sergey, and Jukka Gronow, *Fashion Meets Socialism: Fashion Industry in the Soviet Union after the Second World War*, Helsinki: Finnish Literature Society, 2015 [updated version of *Moda po planu: Istoriya mody i modelirovaniya odezhdy v SSSR 1917–1991*, 2014].

Zolotoy yubiley parfyumernogo proizvodstva Tovarishchestva Brokar i Ko v Moskve, Moscow, 1914.

Zuseva, Veronika (ed.), *Sovetskiy stil'*: *Vremya i veshchi*, Moscow: Avanta, 2012.

Zweig, Stefan, *The World of Yesterday: Memoirs of a European*, translated by Anthea Bell, London: Pushkin Press, 2009. [*Die Welt von Gestern: Erinnerungen eines Europäers*, 1942].

Index